THE UNIVERSITY OF WINCHESTER

CON_{rary}
CREED

A mini-course in Christianity for today

JOHN MORRIS

Copyright © 2005 O Books
O Books is an imprint of John Hunt Publishing Ltd., The Bothy,
Deershot Lodge, Park Lane, Ropley, Hants, SO24 0BE, UK
office@johnhunt-publishing.com
www.O-books.net

Distribution in:
UK
Orca Book Services
orders@orcabookservices.co.uk
Tel: 01202 665432 Fax: 01202 666219 Int. code (44)

USA and Canada
NBN
custserv@nbnbooks.com
Tel: 1 800 462 6420 Fax: 1 800 338 4550

Australia
Brumby Books
sales@brumbybooks.com
Tel: 61 3 9761 5535 Fax: 61 3 9761 7095

New Zealand
Peaceful Living
books@peaceful-living.co.nz
Tel: 64 7 57 18105 Fax: 64 7 57 18513

Singapore
STP
davidbuckland@tlp.com.sg
Tel: 65 6276 Fax: 65 6276 7119

South Africa
Alternative Books
altbook@global.co.za
Tel: 27 011 792 7730 Fax: 27 011 972 7787

Text: © John Morris 2005

Design: BookDesign™, London

ISBN 1 905047 37 1

A CIP catalogue record for this book is available from the British
Library.

Printed in the USA by Maple-Vail Manufacturing Group

CONTEMPORARY
CREED

A mini-course in
Christianity for today

JOHN MORRIS

John Morris

Winchester

BOOKS

WASHINGTON, USA
WINCHESTER, UK

www. contemporarycreed. org. uk

CONTENTS

THE INCARNATION

THE MINISTRY OF JESUS

THE DEATH OF JESUS AND THE ATONEMENT

CHRISTIAN LIVING

Soul-making:

Ending:

ACKNOWLEDGEMENTS

Though the poems here are mine, a good number of the ideas in them and in the commentary have been influenced by the many books I have read, the lectures attended, and the discussions I have had over the years. Though I am deeply grateful for what others have given me, I hope I shall be forgiven for thinking it inappropriate to this little book to add a bibliography.

Several friends have been kind enough to read the bulk of an early draft and save me from some of my errors of style and theology. In surname order they are: The Rt Revd Dr John Austin Baker, The Very Revd Dr David Edwards, John Flory, John Grove, and Dr John Sealey. The Revd Dr John Polkinghorne has helpfully checked a few of my scientific ideas. Feedback from all who have seen and discussed my work, including pupils, staff and parents at Twyford School, Winchester, has been enlightening. But my greatest thanks are threefold: to The Revd Professor C.F.D. Moule for his generous scholarship, courteous criticisms of several drafts, kind Foreword and continuing interest; to my family for the gift of a computer and their expert tuition; and to my wife Mary for her wide-ranging insights, constructive criticism, and loving support. However, where the poems limp and the commentary errs, I take full responsibility.

DEDICATION

I dedicate this book to my grandchildren, Oliver, Lucy, James, Alistair, Thomas and especially to Daniel in gratitude for what he has given me and in the hope he will ultimately be complete with God.

The author will be donating his royalties to the charity Equipment for Disabled Children.

The Cover portrays contemporary communications, through the satellite "Earth Explorer", investigating wind energy, including E1 Nino, as part of the ADM-Aeolus mission.

Credits: ESA-P. Carril

FOREWORD

This unusual book is a *tour de force*. It turns profundities of Christian doctrine into crisp, epigrammatic and sometimes jocular verse, full of imaginative parable and simile; but it is more. Here is the expression of a hard-won, ruthlessly honest personal faith.

Speaking out of testing experiences of sorrow and out of sympathetic acquaintance with intelligent young people looking for honest answers, Dr Morris presents a picture of a God who is no interventionist power but who works from within the laws of his own creation, lovingly suffering with us to create free, responsible persons. The terse, well documented commentary that goes with the verse is exactly right, guiding the reader lucidly to the heart of each problem, and suggesting ways of understanding without skirting the difficulties.

The Reverend Professor C.F.D.Moule,
Lady Margaret's Professor emeritus,
University of Cambridge

INTRODUCTION

A health warning: this little book is not a poetry anthology! Rather, it is a structured journey in Christian thinking that uses verse as a vehicle to accelerate the reader's interest and to carry the argument forward to discover an up-to-date and credible set of beliefs. My poems, which are a quarter of the book, help animate old truths, giving them contemporary life and fresh meaning.

My book is based on sixty intellectual problems, most of which I have wrestled with over the years. For me, and others today, faith is married to doubt, for it goes beyond proof. So I write for all those who have difficulties with some forms of traditional belief, and with any unhelpful jargon used to describe complex doctrine. But there are already plenty of books that explore the hard questions analysed here: the existence and nature of God; his role in creation; his non-intervention to stop personal suffering and natural disasters, like the Christmas 2004 Asian earthquake tsunami; the identity of Jesus Christ; the meaning of his death and miraculous resurrection; the use of prayer, especially in a fight against cancer; and whether death is the end. To be different, I have put these problems – and my attempted answers – into an unusual kind of verse, forming poems that are conceptual and problem-solving. That is, each poem defines only one concept and tries to solve the difficulties it raises today. The discipline of poetry can help to express Christian beliefs precisely and neatly. If a poem succeeds, it can be memorable, in its imaginative imagery, its rhythm, and its economy, compressing lengthier prose into fewer words.

Each poem is given a "Context" or commentary which has three purposes: to give the Biblical, philosophical and sometimes scientific evidence for the poem; to develop the ideas and add background; and give cross-references to related poems so that they connect. The result is a mini-course in Christianity, in transparent English, to suit any thoughtful adult, including teenagers and older students. Some non-churchgoers may find more common ground with churchgoers than they expected, at least in the "God and creation" and some of the "Christian living" sections.

The book is flexible in the variety of ways it can be read. Many readers will not want a study course: they may prefer to read straight through, ignoring all the references, and discover the "story" of an accumulating creed; or instead of starting at the front, they may jump to any verse they like, because each poem and Context makes a self-contained unit. For those who do want a course in middle-of-the-road theology, the Contents put the 60 problem-units in numbered sequence whereas the Index lists the poems alphabetically. As a Lent book, meditation could focus on one unit per day. Bible study is aided by the references and quotations from the Revised English Bible REB, unless another version is named.

I admit that my problem-solving cannot solve all the problems raised, especially those above human understanding. So I offer no easy answers and clichés. But the poems do attempt to redefine the problems and offer a tentative resolution of at least some of the difficulties.

I was a teacher and lecturer for 35 years before I was ordained as an Anglican clergyman (NSM, unpaid) in 1995, serving in three rural parishes in England for six years. My main role now is as the chaplain at Twyford School, Winchester.

The poems have been used in services, sermons, retreats, pilgrimages, and schools. In Religious Education,

English and Science they can stimulate discussion and creative writing. In house groups they are a framework for discussion and Bible study. This book is the small fruit of my experience, working in the U.K., plus nine years in Uganda, East Africa, and two spells in the U.S.A.. I begin with my own creed which has changed over the years and has had to adjust to two family tragedies.

MY CREED

I believe in God, the Father of all,
    who began and upholds a universe
    that makes itself through evolving processes.
    God is Love, granting to creation a freedom
    that restricts his power.

Through his Son Jesus
this self-giving God rescued us and
showed us what he is like:
    loving in life and death;
    sharing our pain;
    suffering the consequences of our sin;
    offering forgiveness.

Jesus died for us but was raised by God
    and now lives with us through his Spirit
    to build God's kingdom of unselfish love
    and lead us, as our judge and Savior,
    to eternity with him.

My 100-word creed was not written to replace the Nicene Creed (accepted at the Council of Chalcedon 451 AD, and possibly at Constantinople in 381 AD). I wrote it for school leavers and parents as a summary of their years in chapel and it is given as a memento bookmark inside their Gideons' New Testament. The Nicene and Apostles' Creeds omit two subjects that I hint at: why suffering is unavoidable in God's universe, and why Jesus can rightly be called our Savior. The bookmark ends with a *Footnote on the source of our knowledge: I believe Jesus is the word of God, speaking especially through the New Testament, which contains a mixture of historical facts, the writers' interpretations, and the faith of the early church.*

GOD AND CREATION

WHAT IS GOD?

A heavenly being he is not,
    if just one finite object like
        the others met in space and time.

No superhuman on a throne –
    incredible to us today
        all concepts of a God so small.

Unlimited existence, "He",
    who's gender-free yet personal,
        eternal Being, underived.

Supreme in value, Love complete,
    external and yet everywhere,
        reality that's ultimate.

Creative Spirit, energy
    The Father-Mother, source of all,
        One Holy Lord, unique "I am".

PROBLEM:
How can I define God?

CONTEXT OF "WHAT IS GOD?":
If God were not beyond the limits of a definition, he would not be God, so this poem is sure to fail!

Man needs God's revelation, so all the world religions have their scriptures; but even with them he remains the deepest mystery. Though my poems refer to God as "He", gender is not meant: he is personal but not a person. Jesus sees God as his Father but feminine imagery enriches ideas about God in the Old Testament e.g. *Isaiah* 49:15. "God is spirit", *John* 4:24.

"Yet everywhere" suggests God's closeness (*Acts* 17:28), not pantheism. God's "reality" is not just a subjective, man-made idea; it is objective. Though beyond proof, his existence will be shown to be a reasonable hypothesis. Monotheists agree on "One Holy Lord", *Deuteronomy* 6:4; *Isaiah* 6:3; *Mark* 12:32; *Romans* 1:20. To Moses God was "I AM", *Exodus* 3:14.

MICHELANGELO

God is the great Discoverer,
Of where creation leads,
With countless possibilities
To reach his chosen goal.

Between Creator and what's made
A finger gap exists –
By definition something else,
With space to be itself.

So evil is no alien power,
In matter there's no fault,
Life's simply "other" than its source –
And there the problem lies.

Behind whatever comes-to-be
The one Inventive God,
Empowering all evolving things,
Brings consciousness to birth.

He does not will life's tragedies,
Nor sanction, nor permit –
They fall upon him as the cost
Of Love that makes things free.

PROBLEM:

Is creation predetermined by its Creator from start to finish or is there a degree of exploration and running repairs?

CONTEXT OF "MICHELANGELO":

The opening and closing of Genesis and Revelation are usually seen as God's planned start and end, making him the controlling designer and watchmaker. If that means God wills and guides the whole, and knows both the route and the precise outcome, good and evil become part of his permitted plan that he is ultimately responsible for. *Isaiah* 45.7 supports that view.

If, however, God endows all matter in our expanding universe with the freedom to be and become, exploration, misadventure, and waste are introduced. So though God is still finally responsible, his role becomes more complex. In the continuing process of creation and recreation he is not only the inventor and repairer, he is also the undertaker and midwife engaged in the cremation and birth of stars and species. We are inside not a closed and clockwork universe but one that is mysteriously open. If it existed by chance, it would be pointless, but a loving Creator would give it purpose, so we may believe he is at work to influence everything towards greater potential, along unmapped routes, to reach his goal, namely "the good and the best".

The book of Job is the classic expression of man's outcry against unfair misfortune, asking who is to blame, the man who reaps reward for his conduct, or his maker.

Michelangelo's fresco painting in the Sistine Chapel has a finger gap between the Creator's outstretched arm and his creature, man. For creativity see *Hebrews* 11:3.

SINATRA – DO IT MY WAY

False love requires you to be slave
To what it's planned for you –
Your job, your wife, your way of life,
No other road will do.

But love that's true relinquishes
Control – to set me free –
Scope too within the quantum world
For much uncertainty.

Precarious, the path of love –
The other may decline –
The artist, too, may lose control
As plans are left behind.

The lover knows he's vulnerable
To hurt from those adored –
God puts himself within our power –
Awaits our open doors.

He chose to let the universe
Have freedom of its own.
He gave up power to have his way,
Dictate how things have grown.

No other world was possible
If Love's allowed its way,
Despite the botch – and better job
Some think they could e-ssay.

PROBLEM:
Can a God of love be, at the same time, a sovereign, controlling God?

CONTEXT OF "SINATRA – DO IT MY WAY":
Instead of dictating, true love empowers the loved one to be free to choose. Though freewill is unique to humans, the quantum world also has an unpredictability. Was it possible for the Creator to give some autonomy to humans without first giving some indeterminacy to the material universe they came from? (Man is stardust: the atoms that make us were made inside the ovens of long-dead stars, all sparked by the Big Bang. This recipe for making our universe may be the only one Nature permits.)

Creation neither proves nor disproves the existence of a Creator: the evidence is ambiguous. The atheist finds a self-governing universe, that happened by chance. Also unprovable is the claim that "God created the universe" or, as I prefer to say, "God created a universe that makes itself through evolving processes which he continues to uphold". That upholding may *look* as if God has let go in order to let things be themselves. His *love* in creation is not self-evident: an observer might deduce God's power, beauty, creativity, etc. but be less sure of his *love.*

The life of Jesus exhibited both power and powerlessness, finishing on the cross with his "forsaken" cry and "Father, forgive them". We can imagine the Father replying "I do forgive them" but is it blasphemy to wonder if the Father also says "Mankind, forgive me for the way things had to be, for unavoidable death, disease, and disasters"? Reverent speculation of this sort thinks of the cross as not only about sin-bearing (as in some later poems) but also about pain-bearing, when a caring Creator shares in the consequences of creation and accepts some responsibility, *Matthew* 27:46; *Luke* 23:34 (*Hosea* 11:1f. adds God's pain at being the rejected "parent"). See "Driven", "Casualties", "Penalties", "Unique injustice", "Compelled by love" and "Mayday for a friend".

PROVIDENCE

To say God intervenes
Suggests occasional acts –
Throughout our universe
The Giver interacts.

PROBLEM:

Is the day-to-day activity of God upholding creation best described as intervention or interaction?

CONTEXT OF "PROVIDENCE":

Biblical writers interpreted history as moments of rescue by an interventionist God: Noah's flood, the plagues and exodus, and so on. But intervention suggests an outsider's intrusions into a closed independent cosmos, whereas a more open world where God is a close insider (immanent and upholding the universe), fits in with Jesus's teaching on birds and lilies, *Matthew* 10:29, 6:26-30. Over the thirteen billion years of our universe, in which Mind has finally produced mind, one might imagine a double agency, God and natural forces, both at work.

Science aims to answer *how*, not so much *why* anything exists. Theology explores why, and admits uncertainties because it cannot *prove* God's existence. The odds against our universe developing as it did were huge (especially in the maths of the "cosmological constant"). Fine tuning happened – by chance? or probability in a multiverse? or by God? In our barren solar system, was it luck that made Earth a fertile home for chemicals to be kick-started into life? Why should an interplay of chance and the laws of science create such beauty in flora and fauna, in maths and music, and bring blind genes to see sense in fighting their selfishness? Beauty and duty at the centre of our lives may be clues to a beautiful and moral God in the "midst", *Psalms* 46:5; *Acts* 17:28; *1 Corinthians* 8:6. See "Michelangelo", "Voices", "Sole security", "Lowering oneself".

GREAT IS THY FAITHFULNESS

The faithfulness of God
            is less his constant care
we trust is truly there
            though we may feel despair.

It's more the world he makes
            with constancy of laws,
where freedom to exist
            his energy ensures.

PROBLEM:
In what sense is God always dependable?

CONTEXT OF "GREAT IS THY FAITHFULNESS":
The hymn "Great is thy faithfulness" has one line – "all I have needed thy hand hath provided" – that is not always in tune with experience!   Is such faithfulness a regular care of our health and/or care of our souls and/or support of scientific laws that make life possible? But "possible" is not "comfortable": reliable laws involve harmful effects, allowing meteors to hit us, and earthquakes to shake our dynamic planet. Psalm 91 has a protective God (like an umbrella shelter) but Psalm 23's opening "I lack for nothing" is later balanced by darker realism.

As Jesus says, bad people can "give good gifts" so we can expect more from his "Father" who "gives the Holy Spirit", *Luke* 11:13 (Luke amends *Matthew* 7:11 but both places say no father gives a snake when fish is requested – a problem in the poem "Mayday for a friend"). Regularly, God sends sun and rain "on the good and bad alike", *Matthew* 5:45. This impartial God is not arbitrary, but faithful to himself, giving stability to the divine order, where our sin is always a disorder and therefore judged, *Romans* 5-8.

ELECTRICAL SAFETY DEVICE

We need the safety of a God
Who intervenes when danger looms:
A switch that trips at once and saves
Whenever freedom threatens doom.

How awkward that would be when I,
Intent on having an affair,
Find he steps in to thwart my sex
Because my wife is in his care.

But cutting in to make amends
Restricts the freedom Love intends:
There's "choice" in Nature for the "worse" –
No programmed life in universe.

For freedom to be genuine,
Man cannot pick and choose
God's interventions – we are not
The masters of his fuse.

PROBLEM:

Is freedom divisible, so we can pick and choose when we want it?

CONTEXT OF "ELECTRICAL SAFETY DEVICE":

We want the freedom to fly in an aeroplane but not the pilot's freedom to make an error nor the plane's innate ageing process. The poem makes God a projection of our need of rescue but only when we want it. Such a convenient God would make us less responsible. The Jews in Egypt wanted God's rescue but soon tired of him, *Exodus* 13f.. Prayer in a crisis is noted in "Mayday for a friend".

DRIVEN

Suppose that God did all the work –
        so just before a plane crashlands
or tumor swells to kill the brain
        He intervenes with saving hands.

Why would we bother to progress
        in medicine and safer flight?
Man's brain is driven to expand
        when God's not seen to ease our plight.

PROBLEM:

What would be the consequences on the evolution of *homo sapiens* had God been on tap to rescue man in danger?

CONTEXT OF "DRIVEN":

Early man was probably driven by primitive survival instincts, whereas civilised man has a more rational driving force, the wish to know. Doctors can learn from what goes wrong, so knowledge of the brain advances by examining damaged brains. But that advance – a by-product of the damage – does not make tragedies "a good thing". Nor do I mean the 2004 tsunami disaster is a *good* means of producing global generosity and human resilience, two by-products of the Asian quake, as people rebuild. So where is God? – he is "heard" by open minds, so some generosity and resilience might be the result; also isn't he a participator in the pain, including that of people feeling "forsaken", as at Calvary, *Mark* 4:9, 15:34? See "Sinatra", "God saw that it was good", "Mayday for a friend".

The problem of suffering is not so much about the existence of God but about his nature. The unfairness of life often lets good people suffer while the bad prosper, *Psalms* 73. The saying "God helps those who help themselves" has examples in Abraham, Joseph, David, Ruth and the "dishonest manager" parable, *Luke* 16:8.

VOICES

As we grow up we hear the sound of "fair",
The "beautiful", the "saintly", and our "rights".
These root in us a sense of "ought" and "must",
Which makes the "good" not just our taste or likes.

What's right and wrong may sound so relative
To different cultures, yet they all combine
To hear some "obligation" – absolute,
To love, respect, feel awe at the sublime.

The good is not defined by God alone,
It's independent, free for all to own,
Yet faith can feel its source is personal
From One who hopes his love will find a home.

PROBLEM:

Is our sense of right and wrong just relative to where we live, or a timeless absolute; and where does it come from?

CONTEXT OF "VOICES":

Morality and conscience are partly inherited and partly nurtured by family, school, and environment; so morality is *relative* to our upbringing, culture, differing opinions and tastes. We will disagree on, for example, the virtue of obedience and loyalty. (Many post-modernists would go further and say *all truth* is relative.)

But as well as being *relative*, there is also an underlying *absolute*, a universal obligation to do what is good, though that good is indefinable and vague. The brain can argue how that central "ought" arose: logically, you cannot get "ought" from an "is"; it may be an evolutionary survival strategy developed by our genes (and assisted by their maker, for a good God would want to spread goodness). But the heart can feel this "ought" and try to obey it. That obedience gives not less but more freedom (as in "Dress codes" and "Ascension"). Jesus criticised the culture that misled the Pharisee to feel superior to the tax man, *Luke* 18:9-14; *Matthew* 5:17-7:29.

GOD SAW THAT
IT WAS GOOD

It's easy to condemn this world of pain
But hard devising one that brings real gain:
  Begin by listing what we most admire –
  The qualities and values saints acquire;
Then ask what universe they need to thrive –
If made too bland will values come alive?
  Without adversity – a heavy price –
  What chance for courage, love and sacrifice?
So Eden is our end, not starting place,
For greater good not bad will win the race.

PROBLEM:

What was good about God's "six days" of creation?

CONTEXT OF "GOD SAW THAT IT WAS GOOD":
My son posted on his bedroom door: "Be reasonable, do it my way"!   Yet if creation had been done our way, would our amendments have turned out to be long-term improvements? Our violent universe is one physical system, one pack or network. Everything is connected: change the world's components and you change one of its products, humans, who would end up as different creatures or not be here at all. It is our present physical being that allows us to experience the highs and lows of life.

"God saw that it was good" (not "perfect") is repeated in *Genesis* 1 at the end of most days – not 24 hours, more like geological ages. But good is drowned by bad in natural disasters which can undermine believers, especially those who expect God to make a perfect, safe world. The poem – which does not say a person's pain is a good thing, even though good may result – assumes that values like love, personal responsibility and courage are good, and a desirable goal for the universe; but the reader may reject that premise.   For cancer, see the poem "Mayday for a friend".

SPECIAL CREATION

In Adam and Eve we can see
Not parents that started our line,
But pictures of souls that evolved
As God lifted man in his climb.

The Genesis "Fall" was not once
When Adam was perfect then fails;
Intrinsic to creatures with wills –
A waywardness, running off rails.

PROBLEM:

What is the meaning of Adam and Eve today?

CONTEXT OF "SPECIAL CREATION":
We are told that creation was "completed", *Genesis* 2:1,2. True, it was "finished" enough to establish the process of ongoing creation, so we may read evolution into Genesis. As man's body and brain evolved, so did his self-consciousness. Perhaps the legendary Adam represents the time or long period when man began to see himself in two ways: made in his Creator's image, aware of the ideal; yet responsible and guilty for falling short of that ideal in his sinful, wayward behaviour.

"As God lifted man" adds a supernatural input into natural selection. I accept the evidence for evolution towards greater complexity and biodiversity but I find it an incomplete explanation for the amazing birth of consciousness in our universe, when "it" became "I". Man is part of the animal kingdom but he excels in self-awareness, in linguistic and artistic skills, abstract thinking, spiritual values, and desire for purpose beyond mere survival, that lift him to a class of his own, with potential for great good and awful evil, *Genesis* 1:26-2:7, 3:11f.; *Romans* 3:23; *John* 16:2, 11:50.

UP AND DOWN

The Fall in Eden typifies
our wish to have our way.
To fathom out, explore, to know
whatever God may say.

Imagination that can soar
can sink to savagery:
Our Maker's nest we can pollute
unEarth a tragedy.

It's choice that builds a better race –
the Fall may prompt a rise!
We need a force to push against,
temptation purifies?

PROBLEM:

Though evil is a terrible master, can it also be changed into a useful servant?

CONTEXT OF "UP AND DOWN":

Instead of evil being merely a legacy of our primitive past, it has ironically often been a progressive force for good, pushing people to demand reform. The Fall of Adam and Eve, and Cain's murder of Abel, lead into Noah's ark and Abram's nation. After World War II and the Holocaust, the United Nations was set up in 1945. Humans are "frail" but they may behave with some "honor", *Psalms* 8:4,5; *Hebrews* 2:6f..

Whereas a crime is against the law of the land, a sin is purposeful disobedience against God's law, requiring his forgiveness. Like a mother for her baby, we imagine the God of Genesis wanting the best for his creation and taking the risk it would not descend into godlessness and futility. Every sin hurts God and lets him down: it dents his high ambitions and painfully shows his good intentions turning out badly. So the Prodigal Son's Father welcomes another opportunity to turn sin into good and rebuild his son's family life, *Luke* 15:21-24, 13:34; *Romans* 8:28.

The Bible personifies evil as Satan (Hebrew for "adversary") or the devil, in a battle between good and evil. Jesus fought against the devil's temptations; he exorcised unclean spirits in a world where some sickness was explained as demon possession; he was accused of links with the devil, *Mark* 1:13, 27; *Matthew* 4:1-11, 12:22-29, 16:23; *John* 8:44f.. Today, whether or not evil is explained in terms of the devil, the reality of evil behavior is undeniable. The Lord's Prayer ends "save us from the evil one" but he also taught that "from the human heart, come evil thoughts" and "good people...produce good", *Matthew* 6:13, 12:35; *Mark* 7:21. See "Binoculars", "Compelled by love" and *1 Peter* 5:8; *Ephesians* 6:12; *Revelation* 20.

THE
INCARNATION

OUR EMMANUEL

The baby's name, Emmanuel,
was not a Hebrew phrase
which meant that God vacated heav'n
for thirty years and days.

Was Jesus conscious he was God? –
thin evidence is seen:
how could he share what we go through
if limitless he'd been?

No, Jesus prayed to Abba, God –
no man so close to Him.
When he was raised, confirmed at last,
as God-made-man-in-him.

It's Easter that transforms the cross –
made God the victim too –
for only He could conquer death,
through Christ, the world renew.

PROBLEM:

Jesus was clearly God-conscious but was he also conscious of actually being God, for if he were, how could he have been completely human, one of us?

CONTEXT OF "OUR EMMANUEL":

Joseph hears that Mary's son will be named "Jesus for he will save his people" so Matthew adds an apt second name "Emmanuel... which means "God is with us", *Matthew* 1:23; *Isaiah* 7:14.

The New Testament was written after the resurrection so that momentous event must have re-coloured the writers' views of all he said and did before he died. With the benefit of hindsight it is likely that the writers' view of Jesus changes. Scholars offer two main alternatives: incarnationism (the descent of God into a fully human existence) and adoptionism (the raising of Jesus to the level of deity). The latter has usually been seen as a heresy, especially if it suggests that it was only after the resurrection that Jesus was adopted into the godhead. The resurrection did not promote or change Jesus into divinity but it does change our view of him, and confirm his unique life (reduced by my metre to 30 years, from the likely 34). That uniqueness is commented on after the poem "Ascension".

At his baptism a voice said "You are my beloved Son" [capital S]. His ancestors are then listed: "son, as people thought, of Joseph...son of David... son of Adam, son of God", *Luke* 3:22f..

With the exception of *Matthew* 11:25-27, the evidence for divinity is somewhat "thin" in Matthew, Mark and Luke including their versions of the trial of Jesus. When he is addressed as Messiah or Son of God, he is being elevated without necessarily meaning he was divine. He was hugely respected but he never accepted worship (until Thomas saw him risen, *John* 20:28?).

The expression of divinity is stronger in John's gospel: 8:58 "before Abraham"; 17:5 "before the world"; 6:51-54 "come down from heaven"; 11:25-27 "I am the resurrection". These high claims need to be interpreted carefully, because Jesus was a monotheistic Jew, keeping the Ten Commmandments, especially the first three. So it is unlikely that he wanted others to understand that he felt he was nothing less than eternal God – see the later section on the Trinity.

A COME DOWN

No man, however good, can save our race –
The rescue comes from God's initiative:
In Jesus, truly human, limited,
A "son" united to his father's will.

The fact – or symbol – of the Virgin Birth
Suggests the miracle of this descent,
But he did share with us a common life –
No less a man and brother to us all.

PROBLEM:

How could God who is personal express himself in any other way than through a person, and if Joseph were the natural father of Jesus would that undermine Christ's uniqueness?

CONTEXT OF "A COME DOWN":

Sinful man cannot save himself because he is part of the problem, not the solution. God's solution involved the mystery of the incarnation when "A virgin will conceive" – here the quoted words of Isaiah (actually "a *young woman* is with child", *Isaiah* 7:14), are promoted by Matthew into an ancient prophecy of the birth of Jesus, *Matthew* 1:23. A Virgin Birth raises scientific problems but preserves the unique origin of Jesus. Its alternative, Joseph as father, makes the conception and origin normal. However, even that requires some supernatural control of risks to ensure Joseph's child was a boy (a girl Messiah would not then have been acceptable) and with a whole brain.

Jesus enlarges God's family: "Whoever does the will of God is my brother and sister and mother", *Mark* 3:35. Christians are God's adopted children, "fellow-heirs" and "brothers", *Romans* 8:15-17; *1 John* 3:1; *Hebrews* 2:10f.. The Quaker view goes even further: "God in every man".

EQUIVALENCE?

We cannot say that Christ is God –
For Jesus won't agree –
But he's as much of God as fits
Into humanity.

A circumscribed expression of
Divinity on Earth –
But that best window onto God
Still shines with timeless worth.

PROBLEM:

How much of God was embodied in Jesus? – was he God, or the divine Son of God, or a son of God?

CONTEXT OF "EQUIVALENCE?":

Mathematical ideas (like Jesus = God; Jesus + x = God; or Jesus is half-man and half-God = two natures) are misleading, if they mean there was something defective or false about the humanity of Jesus.

Is it not more accurate to say he was the fullest possible expression-of-God-on-Earth, the closest a real human being allows? He was not a split personality, but a single unified being like us. But unlike us he is praised as "the stamp of God's very being" and "the image of the invisible God", imitating God in self-giving love, but still "subject to God", *Hebrews* 1:3; *Colossians* 1:15; *2 Corinthians* 4:4; *Ephesians* 5:1,2; *1 Corinthians* 15:28.

The opening of John's Gospel means it is not enough to say "Jesus was God-like" for he was more: it is truer to say "Jesus was God-as-man" or "God-made-a-man" or "the-human-presence-of-God". Yet God's Son still had to grow up: "he advanced in wisdom and in favour with God and men", *Luke* 2:52. Peter preached that "God anointed Jesus of Nazareth with the Holy Spirit and with power [of] healing" – Peter probably did not mean that Jesus was suddenly promoted or adopted by God after his anointing/baptism. If the divinity of Jesus seemed hidden behind a veil during his ministry, the resurrection proved his exalted status, highlighted in Peter's sermons: "God has made this same Jesus, whom you crucified, both Lord and Messiah", *Acts* 10:38-43, 2.32-36, 3.11f.. Compare *Mark* 1:1, 15:39; *Romans* 1:4.

LOWERING ONESELF

Christ's birth required an emptied self –
Diminished, servant God –
Yet "emptiness" is God always,
Not once when Earth Christ trod.

Self-giving Being spends his all –
Holds nothing in reserve –
Upon Creation, ventures forth –
Took risks that needed nerve.

PROBLEM:

To become a man, was the Lord's self-emptying an isolated one-off, or a permanent characteristic of adventurous Being, who humbly releases power, in order to empower and grant some freedom to his creation?

CONTEXT OF "LOWERING ONESELF":

Belief in the incarnation requires us to live with paradox: the unlimited became limited; timeless, timed; sovereign, servant; almighty, vulnerable. Paul describes this in a puzzling image: a pre-existing Jesus emptied himself (*kenosis* in Greek, *Philippians* 2:5-8) but that cannot mean that the godhead was literally empty, for then there would be no God. It pictures the Lord humbling himself, becoming emptier, when God-became-a-man. So we might conclude that "Jesus was God-reduced-to-a-real-man".

Thus the independent God shows himself dependent on others and exposed to life's risks. First as a baby, about 4 BC, who in Luke's version had to rough it in "a manger, because there was no room for them in the inn", 2:7. Then about 30 AD Jesus ended up in "death on a cross", *Philippians* 2:8. But when he was resurrected, what other conclusion could Paul, and the writers of John and Hebrews come to, than a belief in his pre-existence? *John* 1:1-14; *Hebrews* 1:1-4. That supernatural resurrection declared that God had been miraculously present in Jesus all along, before, during and after his human life. Creeds in the 4th century spelt it out: in Jesus, God was "incarnate" (not a Biblical word but derived from the Latin form of the creed, meaning "enfleshed") and that came to mean that Jesus was truly human and truly divine, a unique combination of great mystery. For incarnation see *John* 1:14; *1 John* 4:2; *1Timothy* 3:16; *Romans* 8:3; *Colossians* 2:9.

For Paul, Jesus is the one who lowered himself once, yet it was God's doing and he has to wait for our response (compare *Philippians* 2 with *2 Corinthians* 5:16-21). God intended our rescue before the "foundation of the world", *Ephesians* 1:4;

Revelation 13:8, 17:8; *Acts* 2:23 (and *1Timothy* 2:6 ?). In the poem "Feet first" Jesus condescends to wash others' feet.

The creation and incarnation both involved the Creator lowering himself. Before space-time, he was everything, occupying the whole "field". To "plant" creation he chose to let go of his monopoly and allow room for other things to grow as an independent creation (yet paradoxically also dependent, as his "offspring", *Acts* 17:28). Once *homo sapiens* had arrived, the incarnation was probably more likely: God, the exploring Mind, might be keen to relate to creaturely minds that were made in his "image" and tempted to become "like God himself", *Genesis* 1:27, 3:5. But the timing of this unrepeatable incarnation causes historical problems: today, Jesus would be recorded live, whereas years passed before the New Testament writers wrote down their knowledge and the well-remembered oral traditions about him, *1 Corinthians* 11:23, 15:3; *John* 16:13.

The poem ends in poetic licence. From man's point of view "nerve" would be needed but I have no idea whether God needed it. He is personal but not a person so I tried, throughout the book, not to give him human attributes and passions. But "nerve" shows I failed, lapsing into anthropomorphism, by giving God man's characteristics.

THE
MINISTRY OF
JESUS

ALMOST DROWNED

God did not dip his toe in life,
But jumped in with both feet
To Jordan's dirty water flow,
To share man's lot, complete.

PROBLEM:
Why was Jesus baptised?

CONTEXT OF "ALMOST DROWNED":
Baptism means "drowned" or "totally immersed" in Greek. John's unusual baptism of Jews was his sign of their repentance and God's forgiveness. Jesus joined in this renewal ritual, perhaps identifying himself with his people so much that he felt their sins almost as if they were his own, *Mark* 1:4-12; *Matthew* 3:5-17.

Paul says Jesus was "innocent of sin" and Peter's letter agrees, *2 Corinthians* 5:21; *1 Peter* 2:22. Jesus was not necessarily denying that when he objected to being addressed as "Good Teacher...No one is good except God alone", *Luke* 18:19; *John* 8:46. Jesus claimed authority to forgive sins and called others to repent but expressed no need to repent himself, *Mark* 2:10. Four events that can raise doubts about Christ's sinless life in some modern minds involved drowned pigs, a fig tree, a blind man, and worry to his parents, *Mark* 5:1-20, 11:12-24; *John* 9:3; *Luke* 2:41-52.

> *It was God's will a babe arrived*
> *who had no ready plan in mind.*
> *Like us, Christ had to start from scratch*
> *through prayer his Father's route to find.*

Though his birth fulfilled prophecy and was part of God's plan, Jesus did "share man's lot" so he needed to discover God's will, helped by compass points like voices at his baptism, temptations, Transfiguration, John's shout of "Lamb", and Peter's reply of "Messiah", *Matthew* 1:21f., 3:13f., *Mark* 8:27f.; *John* 1:29f., 17:4f..

OUR FATHER

The Lord called men to follow him,
     a gifted teacher, healer, sage.
Yet mainly he advanced his role
     in setting God as centre-stage.

PROBLEM:

When Jesus preached, was his main emphasis on God or on calling people to follow his own example?

CONTEXT OF "OUR FATHER":

Jesus set "God as centre-stage" in the Lord's Prayer, temptations, and commandments. His message focussed on the kingdom of God, open to all who repent, whether religious and respectable or sinners and outcasts; a kingdom not political but inward "upon/among/within you", *Matthew* 6:9-13, 4:1-11; *Mark* 10:18, 1:15, 2:17; *John* 12:50, 8:28,48f., 18:36; *Luke* 17:21.

Yet Jesus boldly announced: "follow me"; "my words will never pass away". His vocation was to be God's special agent, and his miracles added to his "credentials" to do God's work. He was the vineyard owner's "beloved son"; he knew his ride into Jerusalem on a donkey had Messianic meaning. He believed he was the foundation stone of the long-expected kingdom of God and entry to that was given to those who became his followers. Because Jesus was so different from people's various expectations of the coming Messiah (who, many hoped, would be a warrior to liberate them from foreign rule), it is unlikely he would have been recognised as such unless he had put the idea into people's heads, *Mark* 1:17, 13:31f.; *John* 10:25,38, 15:24; *Mark* 12:1-12, 11:1-10, 8:27-38; *Zechariah* 9:9; *Matthew* 11:25-30; *John* 3:28f., 4:26, 8:12f., 13:34, 14:6; *Ephesians* 2:20-22, *1 Corinthians* 3:11. Christ's claims continue in "Our Emmanuel", "Dilemma", and "Almost drowned".

ABBA

"Daddy" was the novel word
Jesus gave the Lord –
Intimate for Ultimate –
Fam'ly ties assured.

PROBLEM:
What was distinctive about the prayers of Jesus and about his relationship with the God of the Jews?

CONTEXT OF "ABBA":
Old Testament Jews were careful and reverential in their use of God's name. Though the Psalmist and Isaiah spoke of God as Father, Jesus was more intimate, addressing God in a novel way, as *"Abba"*, Aramaic for "Dad". That word is used by Jesus once, in *Mark* 14:36, and by Paul twice, *Romans* 8:15 and *Galatians* 4:6.

This alters our view of God: if Old Testament Judaism emphasised God as the lawgiver and judge, he is more the Father in the New Testament. However hard or little they tried, Israel failed to keep God's law and covenant (agreement) made at Sinai, so his favor could not be earned. A new covenant (*testamentum* Latin) offered the Father's unmerited grace to all people who put faith in God. Old and new covenants can be compared in *Exodus* 24:7; *Matthew* 26:28; *Galatians* 3:6-14 "Abraham's sons" and *Genesis* 22:18.

So Abba is for us too: we are encouraged to combine reverence for the "Most High" with a family relationship with our "Father". The Lord's Prayer (a model that unites several religions, for the language is not distinctively Christian) puts praise before petitions, so we start with worshiping the Father before asking for food, forgiveness, and protection for our fragile faith, *Luke* 6:35,36, 11:2-4, 12:30; *Matthew* 6:6-15, 7:11, 10:29, 23:9; *Mark* 11:25. See "High earners" and "Future past" for how the Father judges us.

BLESSINGS IN DISGUISE?

The human race divides in two:
  The hungry
  And self-satisfied;
Only to those who beg for more
Can Christ address their appetite.

PROBLEM:

In his radical Sermon on the Mount, what did Jesus mean by saying hunger is good for us?

CONTEXT OF "BLESSINGS IN DISGUISE?":

"Blessed are those who hunger and thirst to see right prevail; they shall be satisfied", *Matthew* 5:6. This fourth Beatitude, about the blessing that comes to those who are hungry to do God's will, fits Mary's gratitude for being chosen: "He has filled the hungry with good things, and sent the rich away empty", *Luke* 1:53.

My poem, which is addressing the spiritual appetite described by Matthew, assumes that he is recording the original form of the Beatitude. Luke's gospel has an interest in poverty and riches and in his version the literally poor, hungry and weeping are blessed, *Luke* 6:20-25. The fasting and discipline of Ramadan and Lent may be rewarding: abstinence may promote more spiritual growth than rich self-indulgence. During my years in East Africa, I was humbled by the generosity and joy of those with little.

The Sermon was not all radical; Jesus approved the essence of the law and the prophets: "Always treat others as you would like them to treat you", *Matthew* 7:12. Another of his one-liners summed up a road to "happiness", *Acts* 20:35.

DRESS CODES

We dress ourselves the way we want –
It's smart to please oneself,
But tailor-Christ sells simple style –
Strips off the "suit-yourself".

PROBLEM:

If a picture that Jesus used is less relevant today, can we update it successfully?

CONTEXT OF "DRESS CODES":

Jesus wanted to save egoistic man from a life lived solely for self-satisfaction, so he taught self-denial through the images of a Roman cross, a ploughing yoke, and a grain of wheat, *Mark* 8:34; *Matthew* 11:29; *John* 12:24. To do his Father's will, Jesus surrendered his own freedom, yet he appeared a remarkably free person, freer than Pilate who was captive to political pressures.

"Freedom", where it exists, is too big and ambiguous an idea to discuss properly here. Briefly, we all want two freedoms, freedom *to* and freedom *from*. But my freedom *to* do as I like competes with your freedom *from* my noise, bad driving, racial discrimination, etc.. It is not so smart as I think to do as I like: that sort of moral freedom may be restricting. Not all that I desire may be desirable: to suit myself with immediate satisfaction, I may stop myself from getting richer satisfaction later. I don't want freedom from all restraint (the old yoke); I want freedom from self-defeating desires so that I may find long-term fulfillment and – paradoxically – boundless freedom.

Some wrong boundaries were erected in the past. We learn from the Sermon on the Mount: "There must be no limit to your goodness, as your heavenly Father's goodness knows no bounds", *Matthew* 5:48. So "Love your neighbor and hate your enemy" becomes "Love your enemies and pray for your persecutors". An ethic of mutual responsibility and non-violent resistance (except for his violence in the Temple? *Mark* 11:15-19) is encouraged, so that love can "conquer evil", *Matthew* 5: 43,44; *Genesis* 4:9; *Romans* 12:21,15:3.

ADULTERY

To score a point and knock him out
They use a woman's shame;
Will Christ forgive adultery
Or back the Law with blame?

"A sinless one is qualified
To stone her for her lust –
So go ahead, as Moses taught,
While I just draw in dust."

Accusers slunk away in shame
And left the girl alone –
"I don't condemn you for your act,
But sin I can't condone:

Depart in peace, please don't repeat" –
Her life redeemed in time –
Christ aimed to make us better men,
In dust he'd drawn a line.

PROBLEM:
Was Jesus a reformer or supporter of the Mosaic law?

CONTEXT OF "ADULTERY":
The Mosaic law was recognised as the commands of God which had death penalties for adultery, homosexuality, and disrespect towards parents and the Sabbath in *Leviticus* 20; *Numbers* 15:32-36; *Deuteronomy* 21:18-21; *Exodus* 21:15-17. So Pharisees wanted to know where Jesus stood, and used the arrested woman as a test case in *John* 8:1-11. Today, homosexuality divides churches, though usury (forbidden in *Leviticus* 25:36) has long been allowed. See more of Christ's reforms in "Feet first" and *Mark* 7:9-13.

FEET FIRST

The wrong way round it is, we feel,
        When Christ serves like a slave
And washes feet – that's not the way
        A monarch should behave.

Man likes to stand on his two feet,
        Walk independent ways,
Not let a humble Servant Lord,
        Be leader of his days.

PROBLEM:
Is Christ's style of leadership relevant today?

CONTEXT OF "FEET FIRST":
Christ could not be Peter's Lord without also being Peter's servant, washing away the dirt of sin, *John* 13:1-20. "Who but God can forgive sins?" protested the scribes, *Mark* 2:7. An emphasis on the servant God has become common only fairly recently. "The Son of Man did not come to be served but to serve." Here Jesus uses his favorite title for himself which is more a logo for his chosen vocation. Son of Man avoids being seen as a warlike Messiah who would expel the Romans. In Daniel's Old Testament vision the Son of Man was not a freedom fighter: he was a human figure representing God's suffering people who would all be honoured at last in God's court and kingdom, for remaining faithful in persecution, even to death, *Mark* 10:45, 14:61f.; *Daniel* 7:13f.; *John* 1: 49-51.

Jesus washed the disciples' feet as "an example", 13:15. Humility is not a common attribute of today's leaders: they seem to enjoy power, as did James and John, *Mark* 10:37. Strong leadership (and an Almighty God) has its appeal; perhaps Judas betrayed Jesus because his style of leadership was disappointing, and Peter objected to Christ's service and suffering, *Mark* 8:29f..

Man prefers to be master of his fate, not humbly admit he cannot save himself. However high he tries to jump morally, he drops short of God's high bar of requirements – and Jesus raised it higher than others, so we need his service to lift us, *Matthew* 5:20f..

DILEMMA

Was Jesus mad, or self-deceived?
How are his boasts to be received?
Was he a fraud who lied, he knew?
Or can it be his claims were true?

PROBLEM:

What choices are open to us in deciding who Jesus was?

CONTEXT OF "DILEMMA":

Those who see Jesus as no more than a great moral teacher face at least two problems. Firstly, had Jesus lied about who he was, would those lies disqualify him as a great moral teacher? Secondly, there are many places where his moral teaching and healing are woven into his extraordinary claims about himself, so they are difficult to separate. The Sermon on the Mount's morality includes his own high claims, even to be the judge of all on Judgment Day, *Matthew* 5:11, 17, 7:21-28. After the Sermon, his authority is recognised and healing is given to a leper and a Roman's servant, *Matthew* 8:1-15. (For later Son of Man claims see *Matthew* 25:31f.; *Mark* 14:61f.; *Daniel* 7:13f..)

Healing and moral teaching lead into his "boasts" in *Matthew* 11:26,27 and throughout John's gospel, peaking in chapter 8; see also *John* 4:26, 13:3, 14:1-13. Jesus felt more than a prophet, for he fulfilled prophecy, *Luke* 4:21. Paradoxically, he had a high opinion of himself and the humility to mix with disreputable people. If we think Jesus was mistaken about his speedy return (Second Coming) during "the present generation", that could raise our respect for this real person – men don't know everything, *Luke* 7:34; *Mark* 2:15f., 13:30-33; *John* 14:3, 21:22. See omniscience in "Literally, a man of his time"; other extravagant claims in "Our Emmanuel", "Our Father", and "Almost drowned"; "mad" in *Mark* 3:21; *John* 10:20.

THE DEATH OF JESUS AND THE ATONEMENT

CASUALTIES

All things cannot be other than themselves,
  So flakes of snow can form an avalanche,
  And genes mutate for better or for worse,
  The leopard hauls his prey up to a branch.

If God intended humans with a choice,
  Perhaps freewill is indivisible;
  In everything from particles to maths
  There's leeway for the unpredictable.

So nothing is immune from casualties
  When Love allows all matter to be free –
  This necessary cost God chose to share
  As casualty himself upon a tree.

No other way for Love to be itself –
  Creator pays the price of letting go –
  Such violence intrinsic to the whole –
  Faith trusts him to bring good from tragic woe.

PROBLEM:

In the world as we know it, are casualties inevitable, so life cannot be anything other than a mix of joy and pain?

CONTEXT OF "CASUALTIES":

Deism, which sees God as an absentee landlord, is largely absent from the Bible, where God is a hands-on participant, not a spectator. Jesus shares our pain in *1 Peter* 2:21-25; *Hebrews* 4:14-16. "Freewill" is not the same as "the unpredictable"(verse 2) but the latter may be its consequence. See "Mayday for a friend" for more casualties.

BINOCULARS

The cross changed not God's view of us,
It changed our view of him:
His focussed love goes all the way,
Absolving human sin.

PROBLEM:

Are we seeing the cross the right way round, as an event that transforms God's attitude or one that changes us?

CONTEXT OF "BINOCULARS":

God goes to extremes in not sparing his own Son, intending "to lavish every other gift upon us", *Romans* 8:32; also see *John* 3:16; *Galatians* 1:4, 2:20 and *Titus* 2.14.

The world today has no agreed idea of what 'sin' is, and some people justify violence, terrorism and 9/11 in 2001. Sexual and other behaviour is often seen as one's private affair; it is a sin not to "do as you please" to find self-fulfillment (see the poem "Dress codes"). The seven deadly sins (coined in the 6th century), may show Christians as killjoys who try to stop people enjoying themselves (unlike their Lord, *John* 10:10). Buddhist meditation aims to rid the mind of poisons like desire, attachment to material things, and pride. The Bible's chief poison is pride, a word with "i" in the middle, like the word "sin". This "I" of self-centeredness neatly shows sin as a *state* we are in, inclined to put ourselves first, number 1, not God and others. That state leads to particular sins, *Mark* 7:17f.. What's deadly about sin is its effect – it divides us from ourselves, from others, and God. The seven sins also have deadly consequences: what seemed good at the time ends in tears, as Adam and Eve discovered when tempted by the "serpent" (alias the "devil", *Matthew* 4:1) *Genesis* 3.

Christ's cross may look like defeat; but turn the binoculars round, and it is God's triumphant grace seeking to repair the damage sin causes, *Romans* 3:23f., 5:20; *1 Corinthians* 1:18f..

VICTIMISATION

What sort of God would want a child
    To come into our world
Just fated to be done to death
    In sacrifice for sin?

If God decreed *another's* child
    Should die upon a cross,
We just might nail *that* God on wood –
    Make *him* the lamb of God.

God, victim of my horrid thoughts,
    Was Jesus really you?
You turned the knife upon yourself
    To stop the flow of blood?

So Father-Son were tied as one
    kind lamb upon a tree –
Their perfect, final sacrifice
    so sinners were set free.

PROBLEM:

Does the New Testament make Jesus the victim and object of God's justice whereby sin must be punished or does it portray a unity of purpose between Father and Son?

CONTEXT OF "VICTIMIZATION":

Concepts of justice change with time and have long been a battleground for arguments about the cross. This poem and the next three join in the battle.

The Baptist pointed to Jesus as the Lamb of God and Jesus saw his death as a ransom and a new covenant for the forgiveness of sins, *John* 1:29; *Mark* 10:45; *Matthew* 26:28. His perfect self-sacrifice could be seen as making unnecessary any further "flow of blood" in Temple sacrifices – which stopped with the Romans' destruction of the Temple in 70 AD. Doubts about sacrifices had surfaced long before e.g. *1 Samuel* 15:22; *Psalms* 40:6, 51:16f.; *Proverbs* 21:3; *Isaiah* 1:11f.; *Hosea* 6:6; *Matthew* 9:13, 12:7; *Mark* 12:33. *Hebrews* 6-10 shows Christ as the effective, final sacrifice, unlike the ineffectual old order e.g. *Leviticus* 5.

On the cross Jesus cried "My God, why have you forsaken me?", indicating at least a lapse in the usual feeling of oneness between Father and Son. Here Jesus seems especially one with us, at a real human end, not feeling immortal, divine – see "Our Emmanuel", *Matthew* 27:46; *John* 17:21; *Psalms* 22:1,18.

Paul stresses their unity and calls "God our Savior", with Jesus the willing, planned mediator between God and man, *2 Corinthians* 5:18-21; *1 Timothy* 2:3-7. Indeed, the gospels show Jesus as the volunteer, not forced victim, even in Gethsemane, *Mark* 14:36; *John* 10:18, 15:13.

The reasons given for wanting Jesus put to death included such charges as: "blasphemy", "Messiah", troublemaker "subverting our nation", "leading the people astray" and "king of the Jews", *Matthew* 26:65, 27:37; *Luke* 23:2; *John* 7:12; *Mark* 15:2. Fear that Rome would "sweep away our temple and our nation" necessitated a scapegoat, *John* 11:47-53; *Leviticus* 16:7f.. The risen Jesus claims to be the "Messiah", *Luke* 24:19f.; *Acts* 1:6f..

"The Bound Lamb" painted by Francisco de Zurbaran, c.1635-40, prompted the poem and its ending on "tied".

PENALTIES

The consequences of our sin
        Bring pain to others' lives,
Recoiling too upon ourselves –
        Intrinsic penalties.

Some retribution for his crime
        A convict may think fair,
He wants to pay the price himself
        As well as seek reform.

We want a moral grain to life,
        Where judgment falls on sin
To settle our account with men –
        Make up for what we've done.

If God's the highest we can know
        We'll find him personal,
But not a person, nor a mood
        Of vengeful wrath at sin.

Its consequences fall on God –
        He's hurt when we do sin,
When we put self where he should be
        And turn from good to bad.

A virtuous God opposes sin –
        It goes against his grain –
Yet tastes its judgment for himself
        And takes that like a man.

The penalty that Christ did bear
       Was not what God imposed,
As if the judge sat high above
       The prisoner in the dock.

Extrinsic sentence that would be –
       Intrinsic was Christ's lot:
Though innocent, he shared with God
       The wounds our sin entails.

No fitter advocate than Christ
       For us on Judgment Day,
Absolved, we'll see sin's penalties
       Absorbed by Love instead.

PROBLEM:

Pilate gave Jesus the death penalty but are there also other senses in which his death was a penalty?

CONTEXT OF "PENALTIES":

Jesus warns of hell but not of "vengeful wrath"; God relates to us in personal terms but he is not a person, nor in a temper, *Mark* 9:42f.; *Luke* 16:19f.; *Matthew* 25:31f.. "Wrath"(NRSV) is usually "retribution" (REB's better word): God's holy nature and opposition to sin gives humanity a moral order where sin's "law" of cause and effect ruins relationships. Justice and mercy are both needed: a moral God would not be so merciful that he didn't care about sin, shutting his eyes to it as if rape, torture and child abuse did not matter. Crime matters to victims whether in Iraq, Africa, or Northern Ireland from where the Irish McCartney sisters travelled to the White House, for support in their 2005 campaign for justice against their brother's killer, *Romans* 5:9, 6:23, 12:19; *1 Peter* 3:12; *John* 3:36.

Peter blames his fellow Jews for Christ's death penalty but later blames us all: Christ "suffered for our sins", *Acts* 2:36, 3:15; *1 Peter* 3:18. Paul says "Christ died for the wicked…[saving us from] retribution" and "condemnation" and "the curse of the law", *Romans* 5:6-11; *Ephesians* 2:3; *Galatians* 3:13. Legally, I am responsible for my own sins. So Jesus did not take away my responsibility and guilt; instead he "shared with God" the consequences of sin, including its condemnation, and whatever penalty sin may reap.

UNIQUE INJUSTICE

It's commonplace for sin to cause
the death of innocents by laws;
Unique it was to heap all sin
upon the head of God within.

PERMANENTLY SCARRED

Unlike the powerful gods men make
a wounded God we see –
Eternal scars that share our pain –
his credibility.

PROBLEM:

What was unique about God's justice and about the Christian view of God?.

CONTEXT OF "UNIQUE INJUSTICE" AND
"PERMANENTLY SCARRED":
A God who makes a universe in which pain is inevitable, but avoids it himself, would not come up to what we expect from a good God. But the Christian God who is "wounded" is believable, having a greater "credibility" than a religion whose God is beyond suffering. The God of the Bible is not the Unmoved Mover, a detached First Cause.

In an artist's painting of Christ's agony on the cross, we can imagine hearing Christ gasp "This is how much I love you". Further, with God in Christ, the pain shows how much God values us, to go to that length. See *Jeremiah* 8:21.

God's justice is different from man's: he heaped all sin into one pile and dealt with it, *Hebrews* 10:10; *Romans* 5:15-21.

COMPELLED BY LOVE

God had to take the consequence of sin –
Absorb the pain and deaths that sins entail,
Thus he released us by his sacrifice –
His reconciling love had to prevail.

PROBLEM:

If God is Love, would he do nothing to save man?

CONTEXT OF "COMPELLED BY LOVE":

A God of sacrificial love who actively seeks to rescue man is pictured by the writers of *1 John* 4:8-16; *John* 3:16 and *Romans* 8:32. In a famous parable, the father runs towards his wasteful son, *Luke* 15:20.

All reconciliation does not come cheaply: a price has to be paid, because both sides get hurt when friends split up; both suffer when trying to repair the relationship and face each other's judgment. God's reconciliation with man is even harder, yet he takes the first step. Indeed, it is all his work: "God was in Christ reconciling the world to himself", "making peace through the shedding of his blood on the cross", *2 Corinthians* 5:19; *Colossians* 1:20; *Romans* 5:10. So God is the active subject of reconciliation, (doing it), not its object receiving satisfaction.

The price paid is not – as some thought – to the Devil, or a sum in God's business transaction. It is God in Christ paying, on man's behalf, for the trouble we cause through our hurtful sin, *2 Corinthians* 5:14,15. So when Jesus died, he was both our representative and substitute: he represented all humanity; and as substitute (not penal substitute, paying God's penalty) he saved us from bearing alone the full repercussions of our wrongdoing. A marathon runner that we sponsor, represents us – and is our substitute by saving us the sweat of running for the charity!

God "released us" in *Ephesians* 1:7 and *Colossians* 1:14; compare *Luke* 4:18-21. This "liberation" is the REB's meaningful word for the old term "redemption", kept by the NRSV, *1 Corinthians* 1:30; *Romans* 3:24; *Hebrews* 9:12,15; *Titus* 2:14.

SALVATION –
UPDATED OR EMPTIED?

Most "moderns" make the cross of Christ
    "A symbol of God's love",
And not the means whereby he sealed
    Forgiveness for man's sins.

"The ideal parent pardons all" –
    He reconciles himself –
So that's the model Father God,
    "No talk of punishment".

"No justice can be satisfied
    By transfers of man's guilt;
Just expiated is our sin –
    Propitiation's wrong."

Gone is that problem God might face,
    How love could live with law –
Now Love transcends his Holiness,
    So rights the wrong in man.

"No necessary sacrifice"
    "No penal substitute"
"No representative who saves"
    "No death that was for me".

So what objective was achieved? –
    "It works subjectively" –
But only if example can
    Inspire to love like him.

PROBLEM:

Did Jesus achieve anything objective by his death, or do we have to save ourselves with the help of his example?

CONTEXT OF "SALVATION – UPDATED OR EMPTIED?":
This problem has many answers, so this difficult poem – which readers may want to skip and return to later – is a collection of modern views, putting the imagined voices of theologians in speech marks. "Moderns" have rightly questioned any unworthy ideas of God (notably in propitiation, as if God were an angry person needing to be appeased before he forgives).

St Anselm's "satisfaction" theory starts verse three. "Propitiation" in *1 John* 2:2, 4:10 in the King James AV, is replaced by an atoning sacrifice in REB, NRSV and NIV. "Propitiation" as a place of appeasement in *Romans* 3:25 (AV) becomes "a sacrifice or place of atonement" (at-one-ment, or reconciliation) in NRSV and NIV and "means of expiating sin" in REB. Expiation deals with sin, propitiation with feelings; expiation removes or makes amends for the sin that breaks relations between God and man; propitiation changes God's attitude towards sinners.

"Substitute" builds on *Mark* 10:45, 15:34; *1 Timothy* 2:6; *John* 11:50; *2 Corinthians* 5:21; and the sin-bearing of *Hebrews* 9:28; *1 Peter* 2:24; *Isaiah* 53. "Penal" is doubtful: *Galatians* 3:13 is the closest Paul gets to saying that Jesus bore a penalty as a substitute for guilty sinners – see "Penalties".

It is often said that "sacrifice" in the Old Testament was not (mainly) to do with punishment, so no penalty need be seen in Christ's sacrifice. Many say that there was "no necessary sacrifice"– from here I get my useful litmus test to separate the many explanations of the cross: "Was Christ's death *necessary?*".

Christ's example (central to Abelard) ends the poem but my italics wonder if man is able to follow it e.g. *Philippians* 2; *Romans* 12:1f..

God did not start to forgive at the crucifixion 30 AD. Centuries before that, Abraham was accepted: the cross works for all time, *Galatians* 3:6f.; *John* 8:56; *1 Peter* 3:18; *Mark* 2:5; *Matthew* 6:14; *1 Corinthians* 1:18f..

AT THE CROSSROADS

Christ's cross achieves four ends:
Condemns
all human sin

Partakes
its pain and
blame

Forgiveness
it
provides

Example
it
proclaims

PROBLEM:

How can we sum up what Jesus achieved by his death?

CONTEXT OF "AT THE CROSSROADS":
The cruciform shape offers four lines of thought:

Condemns: *Romans* 3:23-26, 8:1-4; *Galatians* 3:13.

Partakes: *Romans* 3:23-26; *1 Peter* 2:21-25.

Forgiveness: *Matthew* 26:28; *Acts* 2:38, 4:12, 5:31, 10:43.

Example: *Galatians* 2:20,21; *Philippians* 2:1f.; *1 John* 4:7-12; *1 Peter* 2:21.

The weaker our view of sin, the weaker our idea of the cross. If the deep root of man's problem is sin, the solution of the cross has to be dug deep into the ground of man's being. Our deep need is to be accepted as we are; the arms of the cross assure us that we are, embracing us in "peace with God", who "has reconciled us to himself", *Romans* 5:1; *2 Corinthians* 5:18f..

My creed included four ways in which Jesus is our Savior but it omitted past, present and future tenses, he *did* save on the cross, he *does* save day by day and he *will* save eternally. The Latin root of "save" is "safe" and the safety Jesus offers includes security (in the poem "Sole security"), liberation (in "Compelled by love"), reconciliation (in "High earners"), and hope (in "Revolution", *1 Corinthians* 15:19; *Hebrews* 7:25).

GOOD FRIDAY

What is the good on this bad day
When innocence was killed? –
If TV eyes so used to war
With gratitude are filled.

Ideas in books are not enough
To get beneath our skin:
Man needs a powerful picture of
The pain produced by sin.

Though we helped nail God's man we get
Forgiveness guaranteed,
Christ's arms outstretched embrace us with
God's love that forms our creed.

PROBLEM:
What is good about Good Friday?

CONTEXT OF "GOOD FRIDAY":
In the first few centuries of the early church, fasting occurred on Good Friday and Saturday in preparation for baptisms and the Easter Sunday Lord's Supper.

Television violence can make us insensitive to evil, reducing Christ's death to just one more killing. Yet pictures may sometimes demonstrate more than words. Friday is good in its demonstration (however excruciating) that there are no limits to sacrificial love: together, God the Father and Son go all the way to death to reconcile us to himself. That good reconciliation was achieved on Good Friday, *2 Corinthians* 5:18f.; *Luke* 23:34; *John* 15:13.

The visual Last Supper was an acted parable. Celebrating the exodus, Jesus showed his vocation to bring his people back to God, no longer exiled, and this Passover began to be replaced in the early church by the Lord's Supper. In his dramatic cleansing of the Temple Jesus led spiritual renewal, not just inside buildings, but nationwide in the hearts of "true worshippers...in spirit", *Matthew* 26:28, 12:6; *Mark* 10:45, 11:15f.; *John* 2:14, 4:22f.; *Ephesians* 2:20-22; *1 Corinthians* 3:16, 5:7, 6:19.

THE
RESURRECTION
OF JESUS

THE RESURRECTION PUZZLE

Incredible – a fairy tale –
    To say that Jesus is alive.
What transformations might explain
    Why this belief can still survive?

Disciples had abandoned hope
    When women came with silly news
Of empty tomb and angels bright –
    No wonder men dismissed their views.

Yet Peter, John ran to the tomb –
    And so confirmed the open door –
No head within the napkin roll,
    Nor body in the wraps on floor.

The women who had seen the Lord
    Did not expect or will Him there –
She thought he was the gardener
    Till Mary's name he did declare.

"Produce the body" – easy way
    To burst this bubble of belief,
But cunning priests bribed guards to say
    "While we slept deep there was a thief".

Surprisingly, no other corpse
    Was taken from the common grave
Of criminals – as substitute –
    So leaders could their faces save.

When doors were locked for fear of Jews
        The Lord appeared and offered "Peace",
Then showed the "Twelve" his hands and side –
        But absent Thomas scorned caprice:

"Unless I put my finger through
        The marks of nails, I won't believe".
Next week's repeat saw proof appear –
        "My Lord, my God" Tom's faith conceived.

For *something* must have changed the minds
        Of those who saw him crucified –
That tortured frame – yet strange to say,
        Their common sense was satisfied.

Two walkers on Emmaus Way
        Had hoped that Christ would free their land –
The stranger with them changed their view
        When he broke bread with outstretched hand.

A private meeting Simon had
        With Christ whom he'd disowned in fear.
Back home, the "Twelve" were terrified –
        "Relax, I'm not a ghost that's here.

So touch me – have you cooked some fish?"
        He ate it – proof of flesh and bones.
To Galilee these fishermen
        Returned to sail in safer zones.

All night they failed – but did not know
        The stranger on the shore who called
"Cast net on right" – to their delight –
        A record catch that Peter hauled.

They knew this chef whose breakfast fire
        Had fish and bread he had prepared.
One day five hundred saw the Lord –
        Most still alive St Paul declared.

Appearances included James,
        And then apostles – last of all
To Saul himself – church enemy –
        Damascus bound, he heard Christ's call.

But what Saul saw was different from
        The other sightings of the Lord
Which came to eyes of faith alone –
        Beyond our cam'ras to record?

A mystery persists about
        Christ's body that materialised
Through bolted doors, and comes and goes,
        Yet much the same, part-recognised.

His physical identity
        Now servant of the spiritual.
Whole self – transcending time and space –
        Fulfilled to be more personal?

A resurrection literal –
        Objective truth and empty tomb –
Makes Christ's raised life unlike the route
        Believers take to reach God's room.

Or if we think Christ's bones lie lost,
        Apostles knew that he was raised
Through common visions in their heads,
        A presence real, so God was praised.

Was Christ mere product of their faith?
Alive as influence in their mind?
What happened was a real event
In *his* new life, divine in kind.

God had to be behind it all –
For bodies come to their dead end –
Creator's power alone can raise –
Beyond our brains to comprehend.

In Jewish thought, a unity
Between the body and the soul,
Required Christ's empty tomb which meant
A resurrection for his whole.

The proof the empty tomb provides
Declares the kind of life God gives –
Some continuity between
What's mortal and what ever lives.

Though Paul omits this empty tomb –
Does common knowledge need infill? –
Unlikely that he meant to say
That Christ was raised though buried still.

Which theory best explains events?
Conspiracy to work deceit?
Hallucinations wished him back?
Resuscitation? – no small feat.

The expectation of some Jews
Was resurrection at the Last,
But Christ's breakthrough sparked new belief –
'We'll catch him up – the End comes fast'.

More turnabouts for Jewish minds:
> Their Law cursed criminals on trees –
And Sabbaths changed to Sunday rest
> To venerate His victory.

Had Jesus not been raised to life
> Would we have heard of him at all?
The witnesses he did empower
> Saw opposition start to fall.

Why let yourself be cast to lions?
> Why were some cowardly men so changed?
How come the early Church grew fast
> When enemies about it ranged?

The inconsistencies between
> The sober manuscripts we read,
Are minor details that do leave
> Intact, the central cause they plead.

Paul's confidence that Christ's alive –
> As if God too had reached his brain –
Gives anchor 'gainst the skeptic who
> Throws gospel "stories" down the drain!

Unique, the resurrection shouts
> "Revise all views of what he said" –
His life seems in a class alone –
> More credible *that's* far from dead.

Transcendent Christ and God got linked –
  Epistles seldom thought of one
Without the other one in mind –
  Alive his vindicated Son.

But history is dead unless
  Today he's here in our distress.

PROBLEM:

What is the New Testament evidence for the resurrection of Jesus?

CONTEXT OF "THE RESURRECTION PUZZLE":

At first, the apostles rejected the women's "story" as "nonsense" Luke 24:11. The truth of the resurrection is like a big tree: we can cut off a few branches that we think are mere legends, but the central stem or trunk remains strong. It may be damaged by minor disagreements between the gospels. Or it may be helped because, without these differences, we might be suspicious, wondering if the disciples secretly agreed to create one fictional version. Why the tree grew at all, demands explanation: critics have offered interesting alternative theories but I have not been sufficiently persuaded to demolish the tree.

Verse 2: *Matthew* 28:1-10; *Mark* 16:1-11; *Luke* 24:1-11. (In courts, women's evidence required corroboration by males).

Verses 3 to 5: *John* 20:1-16; *Matthew* 28:9-15; *Mark* 16:9-11.

Verses 7,8: *John* 20:19-29.

Verses 10,11: *Luke* 24:13-43; 1 *Corinthians* 15:5.

Verse 12: *Luke* 24:42,43; *John* 21:1-14. Peter is emphatic: we "ate and drank with him after he rose from the dead...clearly seen not by the whole people but by witnesses whom God had chosen", *Acts* 10:40,41; 1 *Peter* 3:18.

Verses 13 to 15: *John* 21:1-14; 1 *Corinthians* 15:3-9; *Acts* 9:1-8.

Verse 17: Recognition was usually not immediate, perhaps because they were not expecting him and he may have looked strangely different e.g. Emmaus verse 10.

Verse 19: For route and room compare *John* 14:1-3.

Verse 22: In the first proclamation of the resurrection (50 days later at Pentecost – which was 10 days after Christ's appearances ceased, *Acts* 1:3), Peter said repeatedly "God raised him", *Acts* 2:24,32 – his recurring theme in *Acts* 3:15, 10:40, which Paul took up in *Acts* 13:33, 17:31.

Verse 24: Continuity, 1 *Corinthians* 15:35-58, 2 *Corinthians* 5:1-10.

Verse 27: Christ's imminent return, 1 *Thessalonians* 4:15f.; Christ as firstfruits/forerunner, *1 Corinthians* 15:20-23.

Verse 28: Curse in *Deuteronomy* 21:23; *Galatians* 3:13. These "turnabouts" were new ideas, unlike "hallucinations" that fulfill existing wishes.

Verse 31: Inconsistencies between different traditions e.g. Jerusalem v. Galilee (compare Luke with Matthew, Mark, John); sequence (Cephas/Simon before the Twelve) and crowd (500, compare Paul and Luke v. John, Matthew); identities (angel, *Matthew 28*, young man, *Mark 16*).

Verse 32: For the idea of Christ's transcendent presence being similar to God's presence see *2 Corinthians* 5:19; *Romans* 5:15, 8:11; *Ephesians* 3:11,12. Some devout believers and most sceptics may think parts of the gospels are legendary embellishments.

Verse 34: For vindication and linking see *Acts* 2:22-24; *Philippians* 2:5-11; Thomas, *John* 20:28; and clear pairings, *Galatians* 1:1-4; *2 Peter* 1:1,2; and trio, *2 Corinthians* 13:14. The growth of this linkage – shocking to traditional Jews – would not have occurred without the resurrection, when God put his "finger" on Jesus.

REVOLUTION

Mortality, a rule of life,
        our clock that times decay.
But new creation came by Christ
        on Resurrection Day.

PROBLEM:
What is the most revolutionary event in human history?

CONTEXT OF "REVOLUTION":
Something new entered our world of sense-perceptions. In Paul's words "one man ...was raised to life...For anyone united to Christ, there is a new creation: the old order has gone"; "freed from the shackles of mortality"; "victory through...Christ", 2 *Corinthians* 5:14-17; *Romans* 8:21-25; 1 *Corinthians* 15:54-57. For Peter the resurrection brought "new birth into a living hope...which nothing can destroy", 1 *Peter* 1:3-5. This hope is founded on the resurrection, delivered by the "God of hope"; it promises a future heaven and changes present lives, *Romans* 15:13 (NRSV); *Colossians* 1:5,27; 1 *John* 3:3.

This radical new creation is very recent compared with pre-historic revolutionary processes that I picture below in two rival ways, accidental or purposeful:

The Big Bang sparked our pyramid:
From apex singularity
A widening mass, then cells – by chance –
Evolving vast complexity.

Invert that shape to funnel life
Converging to intelligence,
Then evolution has a point
And God's existence could make sense.

A GRAIN OF WHEAT

Perhaps the death of dinosaurs
        gave mammals chance to be –
This pattern of all life through death
        is cruciform we see.

So man upon a cross says nought –
        pain happens all the time –
But hope is born if he who died
        is actually divine.

PROBLEM:
Is there a pattern in the generation of new life from old?

CONTEXT OF "A GRAIN OF WHEAT":
As death approaches, Jesus says "unless a grain of wheat...dies, it remains [a single grain]; but if it dies it bears a rich harvest", *John* 12:24. In evolutionary terms, life could be seen as a series of successful mistakes which – in religious terms – become the raw material for progress through God's providential interaction. Death is a beneficial way of life: the Earth's finite material has to be recycled for creative processes to continue. Christ's defeat in death was his victory, though Rome still ruled Palestine, *1 Corinthians* 1:18f., *Acts* 1:6f..

The asteroid that probably led to the extinction of dinosaurs about 65 million years ago was not unique: it is thought that another hit Earth 250 million years ago and wiped out most marine and land species. Yet somehow mankind arrived eventually. All life faces risks: as a baby, Shakespeare was fortunate to escape the bad season of plague that killed many in Stratford. For the risks in creation see "Michelangelo" and the three poems that follow it.

MIRACLES

Most miracles can be explained
    by causes natural –
It is the eye of faith that sees
    the providential.

Coincidence could be inferred
    when Jesus calmed the storm.
The lame leapt up and sick restored
    through psychic power on form.

But resurrection broke the mould –
    defied normality –
That act of God injects New Life
    into mortality.

PROBLEM:
Can all of Christ's miracles be explained away today?

CONTEXT OF "MIRACLES":
Most miracles – whether performed by Christ or a modern "miraculous" recovery from illness or an escape from a car crash – seem identical in appearance to unusual natural occurrences. They are interpreted as miracles by believers to explain events. The exodus from Egypt through the Red Sea involved natural causes but their timing was seen as miraculous, more than pure coincidence.

Jesus was not the only healer of his day, curing the lame and casting out demons (but unlike the incantations etc. of other prophets, Jesus healed on his own authority, *Luke* 7:14), *John* 5:9, 15:24; *Mark* 2:12, 6:13, 9:38; *Matthew* 12:27.

However one explains his nature miracles (a storm calmed, feeding 5000 or his walk on water, *Luke* 8:24; *Mark* 6:30-52), there are at least two miracles, the incarnation and the resurrection, that are indispensable to Christianity for it depends upon them – without the resurrection, the "faith has nothing to it". Resurrection defied normality, so Doubting Thomas voices modern doubts, *John* 20:25. If unbelievers start from the premise "Miracles *cannot* happen", nothing will persuade them, whereas Thomas allowed evidence to change his mind. This unique event can have happened only by God's direct intervention, *Acts* 2:32, 3:26, 4:10, 5:30; *Ephesians* 1:20; *1 Corinthians* 15:17.

NOTHING LIKE IT

The resurrection of the Lord
was not the same as other "myths":
      Not like the Greek or Roman soul
      that is immortal, freed of flesh.
Nor Pharaoh, safe in pyramid,
before recall with food and drink.
      Osiris, after winter's death
      recycled by the spring's return.
Nor Nero, emperors and gods,
returned to exercise their power.
      Nor Hindu hope to come again –
      reincarnation in some form.
No Lazarus restored to life
but bound to go through death again.
      Nor Pharisees who had to wait
      till end of time for bodies new.

But Christ entered The Guinness Book
of Records when he conquered death,
      Identified by those he knew
      yet with a body strangely new –
Not bound in time and space it seems
Man's pioneer beyond our dreams.

PROBLEM:
Has Christ's resurrection any parallels or is it unique?

CONTEXT OF "NOTHING LIKE IT":
The New Testament records several people being raised: Jairus's daughter, the widow's son (both presumably not clinically "dead: she is asleep"); Lazarus resuscitated (though it is described more like resurrection after four days of decay); graves opened. If literally true, these revivals merely extended life but made no lasting historical impact. Whereas Christ's resurrection and enduring unseen presence has changed many lives over 2000 years – unlike a Pharaoh's concern for private survival, *Mark* 5:39; *Luke* 7:11f.; *John* 11:17f., 20:28f.; *Matthew* 14:1, 27:52f.; *1 Corinthians* 15:17f..

The "strangely new" body of Jesus had enough continuity to be recognisable, though not always immediately e.g. Mary (*John* 20:15) and the two walkers to Emmaus (*Luke* 24:31) but its ability to materialise was clearly special. By linking what was buried with what was raised, some albeit strange form of bodily resurrection is suggested, *1 Corinthians* 15:4. Skeptics reject Christ's appearances as just the disciples' wish fulfillment or group hysteria but such psychological explanations do not fit the mood of the disciples nor the other evidence in "The Resurrection Puzzle".

Science cannot prove that a past miracle did not occur. Scientific method rests on events being repeatable and thus testable, but a miracle is a unique event, inexplicable by natural law. So it is easy to observe and prove that you and I do not reappear after death (or walk on water) but how could science prove that *Jesus* did not?

By 120 AD five non-Christian writers had referred to Christianity: Thallus, Josephus, Tacitus, Pliny and Suetonius. Their brief remarks do not prove the resurrection but they add more historical credibility to parts of the New Testament.

THE TRINITY

ASCENSION

Because he is in heaven
He's everywhere on Earth,
Unlimited by time and place –
And keen to raise our worth.

PROBLEM:

What is the meaning of the ascension and how does it help us?

CONTEXT OF "ASCENSION":
Very likely, the disciples did think of heaven as above them, so Jesus spoke of its "dwelling-places in my Father's house" and he told Mary "I have not yet ascended", *John* 14:2, 20:17. But the ascension was not an astronaut's lift off! Heaven is not a literal place; it is, we trust, a metaphorical state of wonderful being.

The ascension is recorded at the end of Matthew, Luke, and the opening of Acts; it is referred to in *John* 20:17 – and in the ending of *Mark* 16:9-20 that most scholars think is not genuine. By not disappearing secretly, the public departure of Jesus convinced the apostles he had gone for good. Were Jesus still making appearances in Palestine, he could not be assisting "everywhere on Earth" at once.

New Testament writers honor Jesus as the exalted Lord, worthy to be worshipped, "crowned". After his unique life, death and resurrection, he alone was eligible. His obedience was exemplary – not a robot's slavish obedience, emptied of independent dignity, but a full humanity of daily choosing to align his will with that of his Father, *John* 8:29. He was "tested in every way as we are, only without sinning"; so he became the Father's "faithful witness", *Hebrews* 4:14f., 2:10f., *Revelation* 1:5,6; *Philippians* 2:5-13; *Romans* 8:34; *Acts* 2:33f., *Ephesians* 1:20f.; *1 Peter* 3:22; *Colossians* 3:1-4. Most of these bunched references support the poem's final line.

PACKING THE SUITCASE

A Russian doll combines
Three parts that fit like one –
One God is shown to man
As Father, Spirit, Son.

Transcendent God "above"
Was felt by early Jews
As Spirit immanent –
Which gave a double view.

Experience forced a change
When Jesus rose to be
Beyond – yet close within –
So two made room for three!

PROBLEM:

What experiences made monotheistic Jews revise their thinking and start the beginnings of Trinitarian language?

CONTEXT OF "PACKING THE SUITCASE":

Appearances are deceptive: one doll is unpacked into three; God may look three but in reality he is one, revealed to us in three ways. At Pentecost, Peter is a new man, boldly saying God raised Jesus and made him "Lord and Messiah", *Acts* 2:32-36. Thousands were converted, sins forgiven, possessions shared, and a cripple healed, *Acts* 2:40-3:16. Saul is changed, and writes "God was in Christ", *Acts* 9; *Philippians* 3:5-8; *Romans* 8:31-39; *2 Corinthians* 5:19.

The transcendent (beyond our world) was now felt immanent (close, dwelling inside believers). The Spirit of God is named the Spirit of Christ occasionally (*Romans* 8:5-17; *Galatians* 4:6; *Philippians* 1:19) but the New Testament consensus sees God, present as Spirit, through Jesus, *Acts* 2:33; *Ephesians* 2:18-22, 3:14f.. (The poem calls Old Testament Jews "early".)

JEWISH CONVERTS

Stupendous change in Jewish minds –
        brought up to think of God as One –
To elevate a carpenter
        whose risen life had just begun.

Now, words of Christ were words of God –
        the two were thought inseparable –
What one had done, they both had done,
        no sharp divide seemed feasible.

TWO MEDIATORS

God's presence comes two ways:
        He's known through Christ our link –
        our Mediator who
        takes us beyond the brink.

The Spirit is the mode
        of Christ's true presence now,
        with me through thick and thin –
        that was his risen vow.

PROBLEM:
The Trinitarian problem continued.

CONTEXT OF "JEWISH CONVERTS" AND "TWO MEDIATORS":
"One" God is revealed as "two…inseparable", *Deuteronomy* 6:4; *2 Corinthians* 5:19; *Romans* 5:15, 8:11; *Ephesians* 3:11,12. "Both had done" includes creation in *John* 1, *Hebrews* 1:2. Jesus, the teacher, did not simply explain about God; *through* him people felt close to God, and prayed to God *through* him, *Romans* 5:2. It may surprise us that no New Testament writer seems to feel any disloyalty to the Old Testament Lord Jehovah by crowning the Lord Jesus; God is still one, and has no rivals, *1 Corinthians* 15:28. So Paul warned Greek Christians against pagan polytheism of "many such gods". He was clear that for Christians there is only "one God" and it is this phrase that is used at the start of the Nicene Creed, *1 Corinthians* 8:5,6.

We might say of great people "Shakespeare lives on" or "the spirit of Socrates survives in all heroic deaths" but Jesus surpasses them: this individual Jesus was experienced as supra-individual, more God-like in his worldwide "presence" and in creating universal hope. Paul pictures Jesus as a collective body, the united church, with all believers *included in* his death and resurrection, and Christ *in* each believer. All New Testament writers join in elevating Jesus to Lord, which is part of the evidence – say some modern critics – of a widening gap between the Jesus of history and the later Christ of faith. On the contrary, the high status given to Christ (Christology) is convincingly justified as an early development faithful to the original Jesus whose life and work began to be better understood, *Romans* 8:1; *2 Corinthians* 5:17; *Galatians* 2:20; *John* 14:10, 15:4-7, 17:21-23; *1 John* 2:24.

For "Mediators" see *1 Timothy* 2:5; *Hebrews* 9:15. "Christ our link" refers to Christians being "united with Christ Jesus", *Romans* 8:1, 6:11; *Ephesians* 2:18-22. His "risen vow" is in *Matthew* 28:20; compare *1 John* 3:24, 4:13.

TRINITY

If God is Love, he must be they,
For love involves relationships –
    A shamrock leaf is one in three,
    But Godhead shuns the clover life.

THREE DIMENSIONAL

Three ways that One reveals itself:
    Creator of the whole,
        As man, who gave his life away,
            Whose Spirit moves our souls.

Transcendent, yes, but immanent –
    That's God at work today,
        His benchmark made in Jesus Christ,
        Alive, to have his say.

PROBLEM:

Can a personal God who is supreme Love exist alone, or are relationships, company and dialogue implied?

CONTEXT OF "TRINITY" AND "THREE DIMENSIONAL":
The term "Trinity", not in the Bible, originated in the 4th century AD. The idea is embryonic in *Matthew* 28:19; *2 Corinthians* 13:14; and perhaps *1 Peter* 1:2. Christians live with paradox: "one God" yet one-in-three modes (linked in *2 Peter* 1:1; *Titus* 2:13; *2 Thessalonians* 1:12); *Deuteronomy* 6:4; *Ephesians* 4:4-6. Man's psyche is more than a trinity of thinking, feeling and willing within one being/identity.

The one Being of God might be simplified into a three-line epigram:

> *God-Father is the Source*
> *The Son is God Revealed*
> *The Spirit's God-around.*

Costly love does not live in clover, *John* 3:16, 17:24f.; *1 John* 4:7f..

THE SCRIPTURES

JESUS OR PAUL?

It was not Paul but Peter who
evangelized the Gentiles first;
whose roof-top vision proved to him
there are no favorites with God.

Paul's mission to the Gentiles thrived,
but he gave them what he received
from those who taught him to believe
soon after his Damascus Road.

We owe a debt to Paul for much –
epistles that expand the faith –
but seeds of his theology
grow from the ministry of Christ.

PROBLEM:

Jesus was the founder of Christianity so is it fair to say that Paul was not only the great founder of churches but also the founder of some beliefs Jesus would not recognise?

CONTEXT OF "JESUS OR PAUL?":

Some uncertainty exists about how soon Paul was taught by the companions of Jesus. *Acts* 9:1-30 supports the poem's line "soon after his Damascus Road". But Paul's letter to the Galatians is different: he says "Immediately, without consulting a single person, without going up to Jerusalem to see those who were apostles before me, I went off to Arabia...Three years later I did go up to Jerusalem to get to know Cephas [Peter]", *Galatians* 1:16-20.

But Paul is clear that the beliefs he "handed on to you [were] the tradition I had received" and "the tradition [about the Lord's Supper] which I handed on to you came to me from the Lord himself", *1 Corinthians* 15:3, 11:23. Paul did not invent the divinity of Jesus: in *Philippians* 2:5-11 scholars think he is quoting an earlier Christian hymn; is *1 Corinthians* 8:6 a part-quote of a primitive creed?

It was "Peter who evangelised the Gentiles first", *Acts* 15:7; "roof-top", *Acts* 10:9-16; "favorites", *Acts* 10.34 (compare *Ephesians* 6:9; *Matthew* 5:45). Paul's mission to the Gentiles is in *Galatians* 1:16.

Though Jesus's mission was to the Jews, he welcomed outsiders including a Roman, *Matthew* 8:5-13; Samaritans, *John* 4:8-30; *Luke* 10:25-37; and, after his resurrection, all nations, *Luke* 24:47; *Matthew* 28:19; *Mark* 16:8f.. See also Gentiles, *Mark* 7:24-30 (compare *Matthew* 15:21-28); *John* 7:35; *Luke* 2:32, 4:18-30; "for many", *Mark* 10:45; *Matthew* 26:28.

From his words at the Last Supper and on other occasions, it is unclear whether Jesus wished to found a new religion – it is possible that his "church" words were added later, *Matthew* 16:18, 18:17, 28:19. He was a devout Jew, keen to reform Judaism, but the resurrection changed everything and disciples became "Christians", *Acts* 11:26.

Though scholars generally believe Paul's writings are earlier than the gospels, these gospel writers were almost certainly not without early evidence, from companions of Jesus and the oral traditions that grew up during Christ's life and especially soon after his resurrection. For some "seeds of [Paul's] theology" that have gospel parallels see *Luke* 3:16, 4:18 (spirit); *Mark* 8:27-38 (Peter's confession); *Mark* 10:45 (ransom); *John* 10:14-18 (shepherd); *Luke* 18:14 (acquittal); *Mark* 3:35 (God's family); *Mark* 12:28-34 (law); *Matthew* 16:24 (cross); *Matthew* 26:26-29 (Last Supper); and Caiaphas, *John* 18:14. To match these parallels with Paul's writings would require an exhaustive list beyond my purpose: one might begin with *1 Corinthians* 1, 11; *2 Corinthians* 5; *Galatians* 2; *Philippians* 2; *Romans* 3, 5, 8, 13.

The principle of the suffering servant in *Isaiah* 53 underlies the ministry of Jesus but whether he actually used that passage is uncertain. Compare *Luke* 22:37; *Philippians* 2:7-11; *Isaiah* 53:12; *1 Peter* 2:22f.; *Acts* 8:32f..

LITERALLY, A MAN OF HIS TIME

The Jews believed the scriptures were God's truth –
      their history book that Jesus seemed to back,
endorsing its authority and cast
    of characters who really did exist.

His quotes implied that Adam was the first,
      and Abraham resides in heav'n above.
Christ's life fulfilled the spirit of its laws,
      but broke the letter of their current codes.

How could that Christ teach science known today?
When genocide is planned, what would he say?

PROBLEM:

Did Jesus believe the Old Testament scriptures were God's word, without error?

CONTEXT OF "LITERALLY, A MAN OF HIS TIME":
Christ's frankness neither corrects nor undermines his contemporaries' trust in the truth of scripture. Nor does Jesus seem to be aware that their view could be erroneous. It may be that Jesus had a private, critical (somewhat modern) view but kept quiet about it to avoid disturbing his hearers' beliefs.

To support his teaching on marriage, Jesus relies on the Genesis version of creation, and believes Abraham is still alive. Elsewhere, Abraham is used to teach about human destiny "up in heaven" and "down in hell". All these teaching points have less power if not one of the characters is thought to be real (*Matthew* 19:3-9 where Jesus alludes to Adam without using his name, *Luke* 20:27f., 16:19-31; also see *John* 8:58). We cannot expect Jesus to have had our modern knowledge and still to be a first century man – can a genuine human being be omniscient and infallible?

"Genocide": See *1 Samuel* 15:3 and *Joshua* 6:17. Often we read of Old Testament leaders who were God's mouthpiece, speaking with the authority of "God said". So Samuel told King Saul "This is the very word of the Lord of Hosts", commanding him to wipe out the Amalekites as a punishment for what they did to the Israelites centuries earlier. Today, we question Samuel's right to attribute to God this command to commit genocide; it looks like Samuel's misattribution. We do not know how Jesus saw this but *Matthew* 5:43f.; *Luke* 13:1-5 and 9:52-56 may help decide whether the God Jesus portrayed would have supported Samuel.

Some readers might want to add other possible misattributions: what God said to Abraham about sacrificing his son Isaac – as what may be good religious practice may not be morally good, for the categories are different. Also, what God said to Moses about the exodus from Egypt and entry into the promised land where the seven resident nations had to be exterminated, *Genesis* 22:2; *Exodus* 12:21-30; *Deuteronomy* 7; *Numbers* 33:52-56.

The poem starts with "the scriptures were God's truth". The words "scripture" and "God" are interchangeable in *Romans* 9:17; *Galatians* 3:8; *Matthew* 19:4,5. Words of scripture are taken as words of God / Holy Spirit in *Mark* 12:36; *Acts* 1:16, 4:25, 28:25; *Hebrews* 9:8, 10:15. Timothy is told "All scripture is inspired by God" (NRSV) but the REB has "All inspired scripture...", *2 Timothy* 3:15-17. Paul's letters are part of "the other scriptures" despite "some obscure passages", *2 Peter* 3:16.

The complex issue of Old Testament books and the canon is simplified here into the unity of one literal "history book": there is more diversity in the Law, Prophets, Psalms and other poetry than just "history". Jesus is conscious of the "authority" of scripture (*Matthew* 5:17-20) even to the "letter" (*Matthew* 5:18; *Luke* 16:17), which "cannot be set aside", *John* 10:35; *Mark* 7:9-13. So too his own "words will never pass away", *Mark* 13:31. He fulfilled the prophetic scriptures, *Matthew* 5:17; *Luke* 24:25-47.

However, in several ways Jesus "broke the letter of their current codes" and criticized legalism – though his corrections could equally be seen as deeper interpretations of the Old Testament, rather than amendments to it:

sabbath: *Mark* 2:28; *Matthew* 12:8f.;

sacrifice: *Matthew* 9:13, 12:7;

divorce: *Matthew* 5:31,32, 19:3f.; *Luke* 16:18;

stone an adulterer: *John* 8:1-11;

an eye for an eye: *Matthew* 5:38-42;

clean foods: *Mark* 7:18,19;

"I say" often in *Matthew* 5:17-48.

The poem "Adultery" raises moral problems if some Old Testament Mosaic laws were enforced today.

THE LIVING BIBLE

No vehicle is perfect – but
      the scriptures give essential lift
by driving us to meet the Christ
      who is God's word and ready gift.

PROBLEM:

Is the word of God the text of the Bible or is Jesus the living word of God who speaks through the scriptures by his Spirit or is it both of these?

CONTEXT OF "THE LIVING BIBLE":

Jesus is the Word who "became flesh" *John* 1:1-14. "All inspired scripture" has authority, as a unique record of "salvation through...Jesus", *2 Timothy* 3:15,16. For many Christians this means that what scripture says, God says, so this verbal inspiration is error-free. Yet critics of the New Testament see textual variations and some contradictions. Most of these faults are, I believe, minor details, whereas in its essentials, the New Testament is historically reliable. Its truths – carried by the imperfect vehicle of words – are inspired in the sense they are God's message, pointing today's readers to a living and inspiring Jesus.

The footnote to my creed says the New Testament contains a mixture of facts, interpretations, and faith. The reader of the New Testament is left to decide where these three apply: he may read all the events as historical facts or he may (as I do) leave open the possibility that some may be uncertain or symbolic, and that a few of the sayings of Jesus may not be his but are later beliefs. See "Our Emmanuel", "Miracles", "Jesus or Paul?", "Literally, a man of his time".

Though the Bible is generally trustworthy, not all parts are intended to be taken literally: poetry needs to be taken as poetic truth; parable as parable; history as history, literally; Genesis as revealed truth not science textbook. Through it all, God speaks, his Word Jesus is heard, and his Spirit guides, *John* 16:13, 20:29; *Hebrews* 1:2, 4:12; *Ephesians* 6:17.

CHRISTIAN
LIVING

TWO DOORS

Between our God and man
        there is a door marked sin.
But Christ who bore its pain
        achieved our access in.

Before I can enjoy
        this entry to God's grace,
I need unlock my heart –
        its door shuts out Christ's face.

PROBLEM WITH **BEGINNING**:
How does one enter a close relationship with God?

CONTEXT OF "TWO DOORS":
Faith gives access to "peace with God through our Lord Jesus Christ, who has given us access to ... grace". Repent (change direction, turnabout) and "enter by the narrow gate" Jesus preached. The risen Jesus stands "knocking at the door", waiting for repentance and the heart to open, so head-knowledge about him can begin to change into a more personal relationship, *Romans* 5:1f., *Matthew* 4:17, 7:13, 21, *Revelation* 3:20. In New Testament times, baptism came soon after conversion as a sign of faith, cleansing, and admission to the church, *1 Timothy* 6:12; *Acts* 22:16; *1 Corinthians* 12:13.

Sin is defined in the poem "Binoculars" and grace in "High earners". Whereas sin divides life from life (one person from himself, from others, and from God), grace turns fate into destiny. Blind fate (that makes our genes, death, sinful nature, etc. unavoidable) is lifted by grace into purposeful living, conscious of forgiveness that extends beyond death.

COMMISSIONED

Not for our ease his Spirit's given
But to empower us in his mission,
To reconcile the world to God
Through witnessing to where he trod.

PROBLEM WITH **WITNESSING**:
What is our job as disciples and what help do we get?

CONTEXT OF "COMMISSIONED":
Christ commissioned his disciples, equipping them "with power" from the "gift promised by my Father", which came at Pentecost, *Luke* 24:46-49; *Matthew* 28:16-20; *John* 15:26,27.

Jesus was God's "faithful witness" and he offers his "ambassadors" some "armor" and big "resources", *Revelation* 1:5; 2 *Corinthians* 5:20; *Ephesians* 6:11, 1:19, 6:13f.; 1 *Peter* 2:9.

Jesus agreed that all the Old Testament laws could be summed up in just two commandments, to love God with all you have and "to love your neighbor as yourself" – not "more than yourself", nor for reward, but for its own sake, *Mark* 12:31. In my creed I wrote that our job is "to build God's kingdom of unselfish love". Instead of each person battling alone with problems, we are called to "carry one another's burdens and in this way you will fulfill the law of Christ", *Galatians* 6:2, 5:14. That consideration for others requires empathy to put ourselves in others' shoes. We can make more of a difference to our world by keeping our eyes, not on the Church with its partly disgraceful history, but on Jesus whose death to self led to his resurrection, so enabling us to die to ego and begin our rebirth into life that is eternal, *Hebrews* 12:1.2; *Mark* 8:34f.; *James* 2:8; *Romans* 13:9; *Philippians* 2:4, 4:5.

NOT FAST FOOD

The wafer speaks of life laid down
Unselfish to the end;
The blood shows life released by death
To rise to be with God.

We make our own the death of Christ,
The broken bread breaks us,
We wash it down with costly wine
Decanted from his life.

The bread and wine serve as a means
To hammer home the end,
Where nailed-down self can rise again
In union with God.

PROBLEM WITH **WORSHIPING**:
What do the sacraments of bread and wine mean?

CONTEXT OF "NOT FAST FOOD":
The Last Supper is in *Mark* 14:12-26; *Matthew* 26:17-30; *Luke* 22:7-23. Whatever its name (Holy Communion, Eucharist, Mass, Breaking of Bread – the latter recalling early church fellowship meals), Christians do it together, in the fellowship of their "common life", *Acts* 2:46; *1 John* 1:3; *Philippians* 2:1. Christ's death was "once for all", final, so the "Lord's Supper" is more a memorial "in memory" than a repeat sacrifice on an altar, *Hebrews* 10:10-25; *1 Corinthians* 11:20f.; *Romans* 6:10.

Though only bread and wine, they symbolise more, and are a means whereby God's grace may strengthen us. The external event of Christ's death is made internal by faith as we eat and drink "costly wine", *1 Corinthians* 6:20. "Nailed-down self" refers to the self-renunciation in *Mark* 8:34-38; wheat in *John* 12:24-26; and the shepherd, *John* 10:14-18.

UNCONTROLLED VIOLENCE

"God's in control", the vicar said –
        but doubts are raised when saints are killed:
His sovereignty is not the kind
        that guarantees all good fulfilled.

OMNISCIENCE

Our future isn't knowable
Before things come to pass –
Though God does know what can be known
Beyond our looking glass.

PROBLEM WITH **PRAYING**:
Is the God we pray to, one who knows all, and controls events?

CONTEXT OF "UNCONTROLLED VIOLENCE" AND "OMNISCIENCE":

"Vicar" refers to a BBC report on 16th January 2003 of his funeral address for a popular detective, stabbed in Manchester in an anti-terrorist raid. God's omniscience, or infinite knowledge, raises the problem of what can be known before it happens. We are told that God knew Jesus would be killed (e.g. *John* 17:1f. and Jesus often spoke of his coming death, *Mark* 8:31 onwards) but he chose not to intervene to stop it. Whether or not God anticipated the detective's death, he did not prevent it, nor Herod's massacre of the Holy Innocents, *Matthew* 2:16. We do not know if Jesus took steps to rescue his imprisoned and then executed cousin, John the Baptist. God's intervention in raising Jesus from the dead shows God's willingness to overrule and bring good out of evil. In that sense God is in control and this generalisation is stronger if we can find justice in man's history, albeit only rough justice and over a long time scale.

Paul's "glass" was a "puzzling...mirror". Whereas God, who does know best, is able to see whatever things can be known, to be revealed in the heaven pictured in Revelation, *1 Corinthians* 13:12.

MAYDAY FOR A FRIEND

No magic is within God's gift.
He does not wave a wand upon:
>The womb where Daniel's brain grew not;
>Brave Joan who fights her cancer's grip;
>One's lack of height or looks or brain –
>Exam success to save us strain.
>Redundancies that firms must make;
>The mortgage, bills, that must be paid;
>The harvest crops that need the rain –
>Though Wimbledon dislikes that pain.

So what can God be trusted for?
>To let all Nature run its course
>Upheld by his supporting power.
>God's influence works on minds and hearts –
>Through prayer, forgives, mends attitudes –
>Such healing of the mind may help
>The body's battle with disease.

In desperation we can pray
For her we do not want to lose
>"Give us today her daily health –
>Though not our will but yours be done –
>The bigger picture you do have,
>And though on Earth it makes no sense
>To us, forsaken on our cross,
>Christ crucified does share our pain
>And will in heav'n our grief explain.
>So we do lift her to your arms
>To hold her through her worst alarms;
>We trust your presence to the end
>That peace and strength you will us send."

PROBLEM WITH **PRAYING**:
Especially in a crisis, what kind of prayers can God be relied on to answer in the way we hope?

CONTEXT OF "MAYDAY":
This poem is a later version of the one I took to Joan (not her real name) some weeks before she died, still young, with her Christian faith radiant, after a heroic and long battle with cancer. Daniel is my grandson.

The kind of God one believes in affects the form of one's prayers. If he is a God who often alters his natural order, one could more easily expect a miracle for Joan and Daniel. The God who shines through Jesus is one who wanted to heal and often said "your faith has healed you", *Mark* 5:34, 2:5, 10:52; *Luke* 7:50, 17:19. Unbelief could restrict his work so "he was unable to do any miracle there", *Mark* 6:5. In his teaching on prayer Jesus promises much – more, the skeptic adds, than can be delivered: after the Lord's Prayer we are told that persistence pays, ask and receive, not a snake but a fish, and at the end those who pray get the Holy Spirit, *Luke* 11:1-13 compare *Matthew* 7:7-11; *John* 14.12f.. Later, church elders prayed for healing, *James* 5:13-18.

This problem – also relevant to the poems "God saw that it was good", "Miracles" and "Casualties" – is clearer if we make a distinction between the inexplicable and a miracle. Doctors' forecasts of a patient's death are influenced by the high percentage of previous terminal cases. But doctors are not always correct: occasionally a patient recovers, almost "miraculously". But "inexplicably" is a better word, unless we have good reason, as sometimes happens, to believe it is nothing less than a miracle.

But like a coin, this belief has two sides: one of them praising God's loving intervention, against the physical odds; the other side puzzling why God does nothing to stop the great majority dying from this particular illness, despite their prayers. So God may appear arbitrary, with random favoritism towards a few. To defend God some might go to the extreme of saying that he has intervened in history only twice, in the incarnation and resurrection. Otherwise, he is reliable, day by day, supporting the material universe, empowering things to be. Were God to be daily overruling his laws of physics and stopping the natural processes of growth and decay, would that world be inhabitable, and could we build up reliable scientific knowledge to make progress possible? It seems that God allows things to take their natural course, letting genes mutate and cells multiply, for better or worse. When cancer cells multiply and kill, that is the way things are in this volatile world. We cannot say this physical universe is morally good or bad; no moral choice is involved; it is just being itself, amoral. Natural disasters like the Indian Ocean earthquake tsunami in 2004 are part of the same physical "package" as cancer cells. We do not know if God could have created a gentler universe that included human beings, not robots. But we do know that our universe has room for patients' inexplicable recoveries and, to the eye of faith, a miracle.

Perhaps that room is mainly in the sub-atomic quantum world where (unlike the regularity of the atomic world with bigger molecules) a mysterious uncertainty rules. To the atheist, an unpredictable recovery would have a purely natural explanation; it was not God's doing but possibly a by-product of quantum leaps. To the believer in miracles, there is a supernatural explanation: faith-healing occurs as God takes advantage of the immense possibilities in the quantum world to do the unexpected. That means God allows prayer a function in the structure of his world, giving it at least some influence to help him achieve what's possible. But this speculation has brought us back full circle to the problem of why God appears to favor some prayer for the sick and not others.

God's creative energy sustains not only our bodies: he also offers mental, spiritual and emotional resources. He knows our pain from the inside: Jesus prayed in Gethsemane that God's will be done, not his own; on the cross he felt forsaken by God, *Luke* 22:39f.; *Mark* 15:34. So we can rely on his empathy and, through prayer, tap his strength of mind over matter. Our minds cry out for meaning so some people think God *purposefully sent* them misfortune to teach them something. I think it is truer to say that if tragedy occurs, God's purpose includes helping us to learn from it and make the best of the situation. We may even discover a positive in the most negative circumstances. "The Spirit comes to the aid of our weakness", *Romans* 8:26-28. Perlman, the great violinist, broke a string but carried on and said at the end "Our job is to make music with what remains" – spoken from his wheelchair, as a lifelong victim of polio.

It seems unfair that the minority – symbolised by Joan – have to pay the price for the health of the majority, so she is a necessary casualty for what we hope is the good of the whole. But the poem ends trusting God who has the big, macro picture. With my micro view I can only say "I don't know; his sovereign will is beyond me, inscrutable" – compare *Job* 26:14.

ALMIGHTY GOD

"Almighty" is a word that meets our need:
Emotions want to find in God some strength;
Our brains suggest creation's awesome power.
But logic stops us going any length:
God cannot square the circle or prevent
The freedom that he gives from causing pain.
He cannot do what contradicts himself –
What better word for God might we obtain?

PROBLEM WITH **PRAYING**:
When we pray, is "Almighty God" an appropriate way to address God?

CONTEXT OF "ALMIGHTY GOD":
Though the Creator's power is mighty, it is not infinite, and it seems he chooses to use it so as not to appear controlling. My creed hinted at the subject: if there are restrictions on God's power, they are self-imposed, so he is still omnipotent in the sense he is free to do what he wills and act according to his nature. His love granted some degree of freedom to creation, which limits his own freedom to overrule. God's providence supports his natural order yet he seeks, with our help, to soften its blows as Jesus did in his healing of the sick. Today, Jesus has no hands but ours so we aid him with our time and money, 2 *Corinthians* 9:6f.; *1 Corinthians* 15:58; *1 Chronicles* 29:9f., *Hebrews* 7:1f. (tithes).

Though the adjective "Almighty" may be misleading, it is hard to find any satisfactory substitute: Creative? Transforming? Empowering? Most Old Testament references to "Almighty God" (Hebrew *shaddai*) are in Genesis and Job; whereas the only New Testament references (Greek *pantokrator*) occur in Revelation and an Old Testament quote in *2 Corinthians* 6:18. Other relevant poems include "Michelangelo", "Great is thy faithfulness", "Lowering oneself", and "Mayday for a friend".

BACKPACKERS

Besides the load of Bunyan's sins,
    Unburdened at the cross,
There is a subtle second load
    We fight to keep from loss.

Our backpack's full of wrongs all done
    To us within the past –
We let resentment tie us tight
    Around our memory's mast.

And God's included in wild blame
    For children maimed at birth,
Nor does he stop the Holocausts –
    Do prayers have hidden worth?

Such massive wrongs I can't forgive –
    Only the injured can –
But where we are concerned, we shun
    The tit-for-tat lifespan.

A cycle of revenge and blame
    Cannot achieve its aim –
Forgiveness shuts the past away,
    Frees man to start again.

All guilt and "getting-even" weighs
    Us down like gravity –
Forgiveness is a better "law"
    For mankind's liberty.

Unfair, perhaps, when we forgive,
    The Hitler that we hate;
But if we wait for fairness here
    We always shall be late.

When I am locked into the past
      I cannot progress make,
It pays me to forgive – move on –
      Relieved by cleaner slate.

It's likely that a healthy God
      Shed load at Calvary –
He would not want to nurse his hurt –
      Such hell, eternally.

"Forgiven people" – that's the badge
      That Jesus bids us wear,
No better label for his Church
      Which all the world may share.

PROBLEM WITH **FORGIVING**:
Why is forgiveness part of a healthy lifestyle, though not easily followed?

CONTEXT OF "BACKPACKERS":
Confession can unload a burden, not unlike that in John Bunyan's '*The Pilgrim's Progress*'. Perhaps what we most need to know is not whether others forgive us (helpful though that is), but does God forgive us? Yes, ends the poem. "Blame", *Luke* 13:1f.; "revenge", *Romans* 12:17f., 13:8f.; "forgiveness", *Matthew* 18:21f.; *Ephesians* 1:7, 4:32; *Colossians* 1:14, 3:13; "fairness", *Matthew* 5:43f.; "hurt", *Romans* 15:3.

HIGH EARNERS

No animal forgives
Its instinct is defence;
Yet humans can transcend
Wild passions so intense.

But man is driven by
The need to earn his keep,
He has to prove his worth –
He sows and aims to reap.

Yet God dispenses gifts
Of grace that's undeserved;
Not wages that are earned,
Reward for time that's served.

God needs to go to school,
He can't add up at all,
Forgives us countless times –
He's unconditional.

A sin repeated oft,
Exploits God's open door,
Yet willing doormat he,
For those whose hearts are sore.

No pardon Hitler gets
From courts that punish crime,
But God forgives the worst,
If wills to him incline.

We graduate when we
Have learned how to forgive,
Although it seems unfair –
Unearned by how foes lived.

There's nothing we can do
To make God love us less,
Nor make him love us more
By trying to impress.

It's not for what we are
That makes God love us more;
It's who and what God is
That makes his pardon sure.

PROBLEM WITH **WORKING**:
Does real forgiveness have to be fair and difficult?

CONTEXT OF "HIGH EARNERS":
This poem and "Backpackers" express the price that has to be paid for all forgiveness and reconciliation. One party pays the cost of giving up revenge; the other pays in lost pride (admitting error, asking forgiveness, making amends). Both make a sacrifice, climb down, close the matter, and move forward.

"It is by grace you are saved", *Ephesians* 2:5f.; grace (meaning unmerited, unearned love) is a Pauline theme; "justified by faith" not works, *Romans* 3:28, 5:1. For "earn" see *Romans* 3:21-31; "sows...reaps" compare *Galatians* 6:7 and *Luke* 19:21; "undeserved", *Ephesians* 2:8; "reward", *Matthew* 20:1-16; *Philippians* 3:14; "countless", *Matthew* 18:21 and God stopped counting, *Romans* 5:15-20; "unfair" debts, *Matthew* 18:23-35; "what we are", *Romans* 5:6-11; *1 John* 4:10; *2 Corinthians* 5:19.

OPPORTUNITIES

The more I look the more I see
Creative Spirit moving me,
Not God as shield to fend off pain,
But opening doors, new sights to gain;
Relationships he bids explore,
To make me better, loving more.

PROBLEM WITH **GUIDANCE**:
Does the Lord offer specific help and guidance to the individual believer, beyond offering general guidance through the Bible?

CONTEXT OF "OPPORTUNITIES":
Personal guidance was given to the Psalmist, *Psalms* 32:8, 73:24. Paul too valued the rewards of prayer, *Ephesians* 6:18; *Philippians* 4:6,7,19. Prayer is more than words of praise and a list of requests; it is the opening of the self to God and that may be done without words. When Jesus had a night of prayer, we can imagine him silently meditating on the scriptures, his Father and his will for the next day, *Luke* 6:12. Jesus is now our high priest offering "us timely help", *Hebrews* 4:14-16, 2:17,18.

Christians might be divided into two groups: those with a strong hold on guidance, and those like me with a mainly weak hold. The strong believe God has "designed" both a big macroplan for the world and a detailed microplan for their whole lives so they try to make each day match that blueprint, *Ephesians* 2:10. The weak focus more on serving God's big purposes and doubt if there is a mapped out microplan. But even some of the weak may feel God's guidance in small ways and look back as I do, at a few key moments in their lives, and label them "special providences" (if not so special to be called "miracles").

Guidance, and the poem's "opening doors", may come through churchgoing, prayer, and Bible reading, but also more widely through friends, the media, books, and Nature. Guidance may become clearer if a person is not passive but actively looking for opportunities, banging on doors to jobs, friendships, marriage, house moves, etc..

Christians have different "gifts of the Spirit" but "in each of us the Spirit... is at work for some useful purpose", *1 Corinthians* 12:1,7.

SOLE SECURITY

By providence the risen Lord
    is anchor to my soul.
When battered by life's storms, I'm safe,
    tied tight to heaven's pole.

PROBLEM WITH **SOUL-MAKING**:
Is anything secure?

CONTEXT OF "SOLE SECURITY":
When we are sinking we have three options: we look for outside help, we save ourselves as best we can, or we try both. Some cry out "Why me?" but I have argued in this book "Why not me?" for someone has to make up the minority of inevitable tragedies. The Christian has the advantage of knowing who to turn to when the storms arrive (as the disciples knew on the lake, *Luke* 8:22f.), trusting that if the body's boat sinks, its soul is safe. However, he may still feel he is battling alone. But his loneliness is illusory to the ones with strong faith: they believe he and they are surviving because the Lord is alongside, or even carrying them. We mature as we learn – helped by God's grace – to cope with loss and recover from events over which we have no control.

Slowly, we may come to see the following as evidence of God's providential organisation: Nature's in-built tendency to heal itself, to improvise and restore a balance; partnership – God's use of cooperative human agents to do part of his work; prayer as an information flow, a way of passing on to us God's superior insight of good hidden potential. Faith of this sort, without demonstrable certainties, strains to see a providential influence on all things in the direction of more meaningful existence, *John* 10:10; *Romans* 8:19f.; *Ephesians* 4:13; *2 Corinthians* 5:5.

Trust in God's indestructible love gives "an anchor for our lives". Extra security comes in Christ's grip on us, as "no one will snatch them from my care", *Hebrews* 6:19; *John* 10:28; *Psalms* 73.

See "A grain of wheat" for death's benefits; for "minority" above, see "Casualties", "Mayday for a friend", and the "God and creation" section.

IDENTITY

A man is not an "incarnated soul" –
a body housing an immortal part.
An "animated body" best describes
his unity of spirit, flesh and heart.

United is mankind in basic needs,
a sameness in his ego and his drives.
Yet persons are distinct within their soul –
the centre of their character and lives.

The soul's a process that is powered by brain
to make some meaning, value, of one's days;
Unique becomes the personal pattern penned –
this essence of the self the "soul" conveys.

Thus spiritual is born from physical,
which only God can separate in death.
All souls alive in him, embodied new,
to be inspired by his eternal breath.

PROBLEM WITH **SOUL-MAKING:**
What is the soul?

CONTEXT OF "IDENTITY":
In Hebrew thought, "soul" (or spirit) means the being and vitality of a person; he was commanded to love the Lord with all his soul, as Jesus also expected, *Deuteronomy* 6:4,5; *Mark* 12:28-30; *Psalms* 146:1. Adam and Eve are portrayed not with a soul ready-made at birth but with God-given potential to be reflective, self-conscious persons, in God's image. Jews saw a unity between the body and soul (monism) and nothing survived death throughout most of the Old Testament (though the soul might have vague existence in the shadowy underworld of Sheol). The first verse of the above poem expresses this unified reality that makes some scientific sense today; but it is faith not science that sees God's essential role in animating and informing the soul's process (verse three).

It was Plato who suggested the immortality of the soul, existing before its union with the body and continuing to exist after its disintegration. For him the soul was the life-giving principle, so a dead soul is self-contradictory.

Jesus urged people not to fear those who "kill the body but cannot kill the soul [but to] fear him rather who is able to destroy both soul and body in hell", *Matthew* 10:28. But generally, the New Testament does not suggest disembodied souls.

The New Testament says much about resurrection and eternal life, both of them God's gift through Christ, whose resurrection was "the firstfruits of the harvest of the dead", especially "those who belong to Christ", *1 Corinthians* 15:20f.. Jesus knew Abraham and Isaac are alive: "God is not God of the dead but of the living", *Matthew* 22:32. A general resurrection for all people is mentioned: *John* 5:28,9; *Acts* 24:15 and *Revelation* 20:12.

The New Testament has little about immortality: God alone has it, *1Timothy* 6:16. One may speculate – developing ideas from the poem "Ascension" – that Christ's resurrection appearances were paradoxically, both in and out of space-time. The ascended Jesus may eternally retain the pattern of his manhood but is no longer reassembling or materialising it in new appearances on Earth. Like God, Jesus is now everywhere through his Spirit, and beyond space-time. Unlike God's infinity, finite man's future "embodiment" is "placed" by New Testament writers in a new location. How we can be "embodied new" (as the poem puts it) is a mystery: Paul says our "perishable body must be clothed with the imperishable". "Complete metamorphosis" is the biological term for the caterpillar's change to a chrysalis and then into a butterfly, so its new form looks completely different from the old, *1 Corinthians* 15:51-54.

SPIRITUAL DNA

When paired with God our souls can make
A bond with him that cannot break;
This teamwork forms a spiral stair
With One who activates our prayer.

PROBLEM WITH **SOUL-MAKING:**
Can the structure of DNA be turned into a useful parable of the soul and its growth?

CONTEXT OF "SPIRITUAL DNA":
DNA is basic to our genes and our physical growth. It looks like a spiral staircase (a double helix), two chains connected by stairs, and each step consists of two chemicals, either "A" paired with "T", or "C" paired with "G". (Their full names are adenine, thymine, cytosine and guanine.)

DNA gives a picture of how our souls grow in two ways: growth sideways in bonding; and growth upwards as we climb the spiral staircase of life. I shall call the "CG" pair Christ and God. Let the "AT" pair be any human being. The "A" is for atoms. But "T" takes longer to explain. Man is more than the sum of his atomic parts: life is added to the chemicals. The soul grows as a baby develops into a person with his/her own unique view and synthesis of the world; atoms add a "T" for *thy* and *mine* (from the chemical *thymine*) as the baby relates to others. For the bonding of relationships is fundamental: each person is both an island and continent, solitary yet social, influenced by others.

So the soul is not an extra box within a person: he *is* a soul, in process of becoming more self-conscious, as the mind and feelings grow to add value to our atoms. For my purposes, soul = spirit = self = a person's identity (a mix of personality, character, attitudes, beliefs, etc. formed in the mind by the brain). Unlike our kidney or other organs, the brain becomes thinking flesh – how a physical brain can become mental, how one person emerges from many complex thought processes, into a "me", a unified sense of self, is still a mystery to neuroscientists.

God comes to the soul to assist its search for meaning and truth in its upward climb. To the atheist God's coming is unrecognised but the Christian believes God's coming is paired with the man Jesus. As Jesus grew up his "AT" bonded with a modified form of Christ (the Greek word for the long-expected Hebrew Messiah). During his ministry Jesus walked a supremely intimate staircase with God, his Father, *Abba*. So that on the cross, "God was in Christ reconciling the world to himself", *2 Corinthians* 5:19. In his resurrection appearances one might say that the "AT" of Jesus strangely materialised, proclaiming a unique bonding between his "AT" and "CG" Christ and God.

My parable suggests "God in the growth", not the old idea of "God in the gaps". Our souls grow with the proteins such as prayer, Bible study and sacraments that bond us to Christ and God through his Spirit. Paul preaches God's closeness: "in him we live and move, in him we exist"; "it is God who works in you", *Acts* 17:28, *Philippians* 2:13.

[Baptism is a close bonding, commanded by Jesus: adult converts were totally immersed, symbolising their burial with Christ, and rising to new life in him, *Matthew* 28:19; *Colossians* 2:12f.; 3:1f.; *Romans* 6; *Acts* 8.38. Though infant baptism is not required in scripture, it became widespread, when whole families were baptised (like family circumcisions in the Old Testament), showing that God loves us all before we respond to him later in confirmation or adult baptism, *Acts* 16:15,33; *1 Corinthians* 1:16, 7:14; *1 John* 4:10f.. For more on baptism see "Almost drowned" and "Two doors".]

Though 98 per cent of our DNA is the same as a chimpanzee's (and 55 per cent is the same as a banana), we are not 98 per cent chimpanzees (nor half a banana!) for we are one hundred per cent human beings!

INTIMATIONS
OF AFTER-LIFE

A loving parent wants the best,
would God want less for us?
Reserve his immortality,
not share some with ourselves?

We need an after-life to bring
some justice to our world,
to overturn *The Scream* in life,
not give us more of same.

If saints grew close to God in life
does that all come to nought?
Or does relationship once sparked
glow on for evermore?

My soul is not a part of me –
a box within my box.
My self's a pattern that adds up
to form identity.

If I am music in God's head
he gives my notes new life,
upon another instrument
when this one's lost its voice.

I want to hold my love again
resume where we broke off.
But all our needs cannot prevent
the facts from holding sway.

For in the age to come we're told
that marriage is no more.
We trust the God of Love to have
some better things in store.

PROBLEM WITH **ENDING**:
Apart from Christ's resurrection, what other reasons might be given for thinking that death is not the end?

CONTEXT OF "INTIMATIONS OF AFTER-LIFE":
If human love hates death's interruption, how much longer will God's love for his people want to endure? To love means to will and do the best for the beloved, however much that costs. God alone has the power to do that eternally.

The poem expresses both the desire for personal gain and homecoming (at worst, selfish survival) with the desire to see the universal victory of Good.

A "loving parent", *Luke* 11:11-13; *The Scream* painting by Edvard Munch; "overturn" – compare the hope that strengthens people to endure suffering and "those wild beasts at Ephesus", *1 Corinthians* 15:32; the Christian hope is not prolongation of this life or "more of same", but a transformation, allowing all creation with unfulfilled potential to blossom, *Romans* 8:19f..

"Box" – there is no evidence for an imperishable spirit located somewhere within our bodies; "pattern" and "another instrument"– compare Paul's heavenly pattern and spiritual body with Christ's teaching that "marriage is no more", *1 Corinthians* 15:35-57, *Luke* 20:27-38. [For Christ's confidence in "going back to God", *John* 13:3, 12:25,26; for Paul's confidence about being "with Christ" in "ages to come", *Philippians* 1:21-24; *Ephesians* 2:6,7.]

The poem ends in mystery: if we don't know *what* happens, we can still have faith in *who* receives us, into a heaven where God is the centre, not ourselves and our wishes.

FUTURE PAST

I have already died –
It happened by God's grace
When Jesus bore the sins
Of all the human race.
We crossed the Jordan then –
What worse is there to face?

PROBLEM WITH **ENDING**:
Should the Christian live in fear of the Last Judgment?

CONTEXT OF "FUTURE PAST":
The River Jordan had to be crossed by the Jews to enter the promised land. That crossing meant the death of their life of slavery in Egypt and the start of a new life, *Numbers* 33:51. In Revelation's judgment scene there is a "river of the water of life...flowing from the throne of God and of the Lamb". In the "new heaven...There shall be an end to death and...pain" *Revelation* 22:1, 21:4.

Christ's death – his Jordan crossing – was in effect ours too: "one man died for all and therefore all mankind has died...so that those who live should cease to live for themselves". His death on our behalf begins our new life. "Since we have now been justified by Christ's sacrificial death, we shall...be saved through him from final retribution", *2 Corinthians* 5:14f., *Romans* 5:9.

In simple terms, God is merciful and accepts the unworthy as worthy of heaven. Paul's legal mind expands this: God justifies (acquits) those who repent; he cancels the charges, forgives, and clothes the unrighteous with an undeserved righteousness. So we can have "confidence on the day of judgment" without "fear", *Romans* 5:1-9, 3:24-28, 8:1f.; *Galatians* 2:16; *1 John* 4:10-18; *Philippians* 3:9.

Though faith is what saves, our conduct matters; in older terms, *justification* (acquittal) gifted *to* us must be seen *in* us in *sanctification* (holy lives). Given Christ's righteousness, we must act Christlike and Jesus says our charity will be judged. For we are accountable, "answerable to God": at " the tribunal of Christ" each of us will "receive what is due to him for his conduct", *Romans* 14:10f.; *2 Corinthians* 5:10; *Luke* 16:19f.; *Matthew* 25:31f.; *Romans* 4:22f.; *Revelation* 20:12, 21:27.

BIG OR SMALL

Big Bang is how it all began –
Then Jesus burst our cosmic grave.
Through him the dead will wake at last,
Remade as proof his love does save.

Yet Paul asserts that "death is gain" –
"Depart and be with Christ" was how
The Lord assured the dying thief –
Not bliss deferred but almost now.

PROBLEM WITH **ENDING**:

At death, are Christians at once conscious of being with their Lord or is there a time-lapse spent in peaceful sleep, awaiting a more general resurrection?

CONTEXT OF "BIG OR SMALL":

The poem's first verse suggests a lapse of time, with one Big Rise of the dead on Christ's return at the End. This is the standard New Testament view, a two-stage process. Firstly, unconscious sleep ("die" means literally "sleep" in the Greek, *1 Corinthians* 15:51) during which intermediate stage Paul would not be aware of any delay, so the stage two Big Rise will feel like an immediate resurrection, a remake of the whole self (after the pattern of Christ's "bodily" resurrection).

But the New Testament is not straightforward here: it also supports my second verse giving a union with God on a small scale as each person dies. Paul thought "death is gain" to "be with Christ" and Jesus promised "today..with me in Paradise". This changes death's sleep into more positive awareness, prior to the Big Rise, and this undelayed bliss can give greater comfort at funerals. In both verses, but easier to see in the second, one's self continues after death, God still loves us, and we are alive in him, *Philippians* 1:21f.; *Luke* 23:43; *Mark* 12:26f.; *John* 11:25.

If there is "time" and development in eternity, it is likely to be different from ours. So though we all die at different times, it is conceivable that we all arrive at the Resurrection together (a united climax that excludes the idea of the solitary Christian, aloof from this solidarity!). Our sun's death is a long way off so the Earth's "cosmic grave" is distant – unless the One behind the Big Bang causes a Big Rise to eternal dimensions sooner. Compare *1 Thessalonians* 4:13f. with *2 Peter* 3:3f..

THE SECOND COMING

Thy kingdom comes complete
When Christ is shown to reign
Not on mere Earth –
This Judge of all
Delivers *cosmic* gain.

PROBLEM WITH **ENDING**:
What is the meaning of "He shall come again with glory"
(Nicene Creed)?

CONTEXT OF "THE SECOND COMING":
Though Jesus did not know the exact date, his followers expected his early return to this Earth, supported by several parables and by the Son of Man references to the day of the Lord coming in glory, vindicated at last, *Mark* 13:30-33; *Matthew* 24-26; *John* 14, 16:16; *Acts* 1:3-11. But the delayed return led writers to a longer time-scale. Compare *1 Thessalonians* 4:13-18; *1 Corinthians* 15:51; *Philippians* 1:6, 3:20-4:5; *Romans* 13:11,12 with *2 Corinthians* 5:1f., *2 Peter* 3:3f..

The return of Christ (for "a second time" in the unusual literal sense of *Hebrews* 9:28, 10:25f.) is devotional picture language for the eventual universal recognition of his sovereignty and the judgment that involves, *2 Thessalonians* 1:7-10; *1 Thessalonians* 1:10.

Though today we are less Earth-bound, we share the same hope of a fulfillment of God's purposes when we pray The Lord's Prayer "your kingdom come". Though that kingdom comes progressively as the early church grows, the New Testament writers pin their confidence not only on gradual advance but on God's sudden intervention that alone will achieve it fully.

Belief in this divine climax satisfies the need to see a purpose in history. On Earth, nothing lasts, including the planet itself, so any reign here by Christ would be impermanent. The far-sighted writer of Revelation sees "a new heaven and a new earth". Then, the Lord is the cosmic victor, with "the universe...a unity in Christ", *Revelation* 21:1-4; *Ephesians* 1:10; *Colossians* 2:15; *Romans* 8:21; *1 Corinthians* 15:24f.; *Philippians* 2:10,11; *Hebrews* 2:14f..

EXCEPT BY ME

All gurus teach us what is good for man
And Christ gave no distinctive moral code –
Unique he was to live it out and die,
Endorsed by God on resurrection's road.

But other faiths take different routes to God
Yet he is fair, commending all of those
Who stand for what Christ stood, and mercy seek –
Christ's brothers, underneath, the Father knows.

PROBLEM WITH **ENDING**:
Is Christ the only Savior?

CONTEXT OF "EXCEPT BY ME":
Enlightenment – a particularly Buddhist goal – is probably what many people seek, each in their different ways. This pluralism or multi-track comes up against what looks like Christ's single track: "I am the way, the truth and the life; no one comes to the Father except by me", *John* 14:6, 3:16f.. Peter preached "There is no salvation through anyone else", *Acts* 4:12, and others wrote *2 Thessalonians* 1:8; *Hebrews* 1:1,2. The poem expresses Peter's point in a different way: what Jesus stood for is the judgment test for all mankind, because he is the highest revelation of truth, our spiritual Everest. Uniquely, "in Christ God was reconciling the world to himself", *2 Corinthians* 5:19 NRSV. But there are many other peaks that challenge the climber so to preach about Everest is not to belittle the others. Wherever truth is found, in other religions or in humanism, it deserves respect, and this more inclusive view was endorsed by the Second Vatican Council 1965. Millions have either never heard of Jesus, or misunderstood him, or walked by him. In God's eyes, many of Christ's brothers underneath may well be those who sincerely practise a different religion and follow the light they have: "Whoever does the will of God is my brother and sister", *Mark* 3:35.

A large God will have large purposes for all. He is the fairest judge of all human destinies. But the command to be Christian missionaries remains strong, *Matthew* 28:19; *Mark* 16:15f.. Jesus clearly taught the crucial importance of making the right choices in one's lifetime; God's love is universal so he "sent his Son...that through him the world might be saved" and "justly judged", *John* 3:17,36; *Acts* 17:31; *1 Timothy* 2:3f.. We do not know if those who reject Jesus will be given further choices, after death, once their eyes have been opened. People will not be pushed into the Christian heaven against their freewill: by definition, true love does not force itself on anyone. So hell is man-made by a person's choice to be absent from God's goodness (though 2 *Thessalonians* 1:8-10 is darker: "the Lord Jesus...will mete out punishment"). Graphic New Testament references show the pain of that separation, in fire, or darkness or wailing, *Mark* 9: 43; *Matthew* 7:23, 8:12, 13:50, 22:13, 25:30f.; *2 Peter* 2:17; *Jude* 13.

It was not a difference in faith but in compassion that led to the rich man being in Hades (Greek underworld) and the poor dead man being comforted by Abraham – a parable that Peter probably knew, *Luke* 16:19-31. Jesus told a lawyer he "will have life" eternal, if he completely followed the law of loving God and his neighbor, *Luke* 10:28; *Matthew* 7:23. Love for its own sake is the best of motives, not to escape hell or earn heaven. [Nearly all the Old Testament was written without a belief in heaven and its rewards, so ancient Judaism had other motives. Today, rewards have their place as good motivators and fitting conclusions: the hard-worker deserves the proper reward in her exam results or job promotion, and the lover wins the beloved.]

A CHAPLAIN'S JOB

It's "Manners maketh man" we're told
By famous College down the road.
Do Twyford think I want from them
Just good behavior, free from sin?

I could exhort them all my days
To virtue, kindness, good displays.
Yet that is only half the job
If I forget my aim on God.

Creator God could robots make
Command our worship for his sake.
He chose instead to give up power
And live like man, outside his tower.

"Your will be done on earth" Christ taught –
This simple prayer summed up his thought.
God's kingdom is the here and now
In hearts that to the Lord do bow.

But did God reign in Palestine
When Caesar's armies marched in time?
They killed all those who spoiled the peace –
Though Pilate wanted Christ's release.

The crowd that watched the Master die
Included mockers who did cry:
"You saved some others and did good,
Why not yourself?   Get off this wood!"

This God in Jesus chose the cross –
Would not come down to show who's boss;
Forgave the men who put him there
And told the thief not to despair.

Sad lamb of God in sacrifice
For sin that holds us all in vice;
A sight to win our love and tears
Not force our will to bend to fears.

Self-giving God surrenders power
Unto his love from hour to hour.
So Twyford hearts can let him reign
If they will only do the same.

Do not expect this God to save
You from all ills this side of grave;
But rest assured he's on your side
So in his love you can abide.

*refers to Winchester College, a boys' public school in
England that opened in 1394.

ENDPIECE

Sixty intellectual problems have been briefly explored in this short book. But all *thinking* about God is incomplete unless it leads into *loving* him and one's neighbor.

INDEX OF POEMS